CRUSH
ON NIAGARA
THE DEFINITIVE WINE TOUR GUIDE
ANDREW BROOKS

whitecap

EDITED BY Marial Shea
PROOFREAD BY Sonnet Force and Nelles Hamilton
COVER AND INTERIOR DESIGN BY Stacey Noyes / LuzForm Design
MAP BY Eric Leinberger

LIBRARY AND ARCHIVES CANADA CATALOGUING IN PUBLICATION
Brooks, Andrew
    Crush on Niagara / Andrew Brooks.

Includes index.
ISBN 1-55285-660-7

    1. Wineries—Ontario—Niagara Peninsula—Guidebooks. 2. Wine
and wine making—Ontario—Niagara Peninsula. 3. Niagara Peninsula
(Ont.)—Guidebooks. I. Title.

TP559.C3B76 2005   663'.2'00971338
C2005-902021-0

The publisher acknowledges the support of the Canada Council for the Arts and the
Cultural Services Branch of the Government of British Columbia for our publishing
program. We acknowledge the financial support of the Government of Canada through
the Book Publishing Industry Development Program for our publishing activities.

Printed in Canada

This work would not have been possible without the support and dedication of my best friend, Christina. Thank you to winemaker Rick Small for my inspiration and to Richard Harvey for my education.

To my dear friends and family who have supported me all this way.

NIL NISI OPTIMUM.

CONTENTS

THE
NIAGARA
WINE INDUSTRY

OUR WINE PAST, PRESENT AND FUTURE

WELCOME TO NIAGARA WINE COUNTRY. THE NIAGARA PENINSULA PRODUCES more wine grapes than any other region in Canada. From Grimsby to Niagara-on-the-Lake, this 40-kilometre stretch of land represents approximately 16,000 acres of vines, with hundreds of new vineyards being planted annually. Despite its small size, Niagara is home to more than 50 wineries. This makes Niagara the most densely concentrated winery location in Canada. The industry ranges from small boutique wineries producing less than 1,000 cases each year to publicly traded corporations steadily approaching 1,000,000-case production. Niagara is fast becoming an international wine destination.

Niagara's culinary experiences are also starting to attract international attention. Cooking schools and fine restaurants feature the best of local ingredients from the "banana belt of the North." This guide has been designed to help you make the most of your wineland journey, with the

essential information you'll need to enjoy this extraordinary food and wine destination.

To fully appreciate the achievements of Niagara's wine industry, it's important to understand the area's geographical and historical context. In geographical terms, Niagara is defined by Lake Ontario and the Niagara Escarpment. Thousands of years ago, the land below the Niagara Escarpment was the lakebed of ancient Lake Iroquois. This has presented exciting opportunities for today's wine growers because the retreating glaciers left behind rich fossil and mineral deposits that play a vital role in defining the character of Niagara wine grapes and, inevitably, the quality of wine that ends up in your glass.

Early settlers to the region cultivated vineyards of the native *vitis labrusca* grape varieties (such as Concord). This hearty and vigorous vine could easily withstand the extreme heat, humidity and winter cold,

producing consistent quality. From the mid-1800s to the mid-1900s, these varieties were the staple for wine production of "Canadian" imitation Champagne, Sherry and Port. In the 1960s and 1970s, pioneer grape-growing families, such as Pennachetti, Lenko, Ziraldo and Bosc, focused their efforts on production of the noble *vitis vinifera* (such as Chardonnay), which make superior wines. Vinifera are much more difficult to grow successfully in a continental cool climate. With the number of frost-free days required for the vine's fruit to be ripe at harvest, Niagara's shorter growing season creates great challenges for today's wine grower.

Between 1988 and 1991, the groundwork for today's winemaking industry was set into place. The Vintners Quality Alliance was formed to guarantee quality to the consumer, and approximately 8,000 acres of hybrid and native grape varieties were removed and replanted with vinifera varieties. Vinifera now account for more than 55 percent of vineyards in the region. This number is expected to grow as demand for high-quality VQA Canadian wine increases.

The future of the Niagara wine industry is bright, with many new and exciting winery projects on the horizon. With this capacity for thousands of new vineyard acres, the greater volume of high-quality wines that will be available to consumers will no doubt increase the market share of Ontario wine from its current 40 percent. Grape varietal and rootstock selection, vine-training systems and new harvesting technology will all play a vital role in improving the quality and value of the Niagara wine on your kitchen table.

Millions of dollars are being invested in the industry, not only in new vineyard plantings but in production technology as well. Although less romantic than boutique wineries, large, modern wineries are packed full of equipment designed to add more depth and complexity to wine produced in larger volume. Barrels coopered from Canadian oak are starting to find their way into winery cellars, helping winemakers define the true character of Niagara wines. And then there's controversial experimentation in replacing natural cork with synthetic and screw cap closures that's still being debated.

Perhaps Niagara's most exciting assets are the educational programs training the next generation of winemakers emerging from Brock University and Niagara College. Most of the region's winemakers, and arguably some of its best, began their careers not at school but tending vineyards and cleaning fermentation tanks. This hard work and experience has formed the backbone of today's winemaking industry. Niagara's next generation of winemakers, armed with the knowledge and experience of old-world techniques combined with the finest new-world technology, will meet the future demand of Niagara's growing wine industry.

NIAGARA
TERROIR

WHAT IS TERROIR? THE ANSWER IS COMPLEX. THERE IS NO COMPARABLE English word for this expression. This French term sums up all the aspects of climate, geology and culture that affect a specific vineyard site. That sounds simple enough, but as you peel back the layers, this concept becomes quite intricate. Terroir is the soul of a vineyard. It is what differentiates the fruit character from one vineyard to another just metres away, even as near as the other side of the street.

There are two main reasons that the delicate *vitis vinifera* grapevines (such as Chardonnay) can survive our extremely cold winters at all: Lake Ontario and the Niagara Escarpment. As air patterns move across the lake in winter, the air picks up the stored heat from this large body of water and is pushed up the Escarpment. This air mass is met by dense, heavier, cold air moving off the top of the Escarpment. This cold air traps the warmer air below it. However, the cold air eventually finds

its way to low spots on the plains below the Escarpment. The extremely cold winters of 2002/03 and 2003/04, after a decade of mild winter conditions, have started to define the region's protected vineyard locations.

The idea that vineyards only a few hundred metres apart can experience totally different airflow patterns, soil structure, ground moisture and sun exposure can be a thorny concept to grasp. Niagara, although considered a single winemaking region, has two very different macroclimates: one surrounding the vineyards of Niagara-on-the-Lake and the other around the vineyards along the Escarpment, near the villages of Beamsville, Vineland and Jordan, known as Twenty Valley. Within these macroclimates exist separate mesoclimates differentiated by slope, air and moisture drainage, distance to Lake Ontario and soil content. And further, within these mesoclimates are microclimates that affect different grapevines of the same variety in one vineyard location. Proximity to a creek, roadway or metal trellising post can have its effect on one specific plant over another. This is only the tip of the terrior iceberg.

The soils of Niagara-on-the-Lake are an ancient lakebed, consisting mostly of sandy loam. Vines must be trained to control the vigorous growth natural to this fertile soil. Twenty Valley soils are ancient lakeshores consisting of higher amounts of clay and limestone, known to some local farmers as "the dreaded Grimsby Red." This soil tends to retain more moisture, making expensive under-draining techniques necessary.

Heat and sunshine over the growing season are extremely important to grape ripeness at harvest time. The vineyards of the Twenty Valley are north-facing, at a higher elevation, collecting less heat units than vineyard plains of Niagara-on-the-Lake. However, the greater heat at the lower elevation also has its downside: the plains below St. David's in Niagara-on-the-Lake also trap cold air. This is why, as you drive between the Old Town and York Road, you will see small wind machines amongst vineyards, used not to generate power but to circulate air. When late spring frost, early winter frost, or extremely cold winter nights are forecast, the machines are turned on. These wind machines pull warmer air above the vineyard in and amongst the vines. They have the capacity to raise vineyard temperatures to 4 to 5 degrees Celsius (39 to 41 F). Each machine can protect a 10-acre parcel and costs more than $35,000 (Cdn) to install.

All of these factors influence the grape quality and, inevitably, Niagara's reputation as a quality wine-producing region. Sip away and discover the heart of Niagara's terroir for yourself.

HOW WINE IS
MADE IN NIAGARA

NIAGARA'S MODERN WINE INDUSTRY IS ONLY 25 YEARS YOUNG. NIAGARA grape growers and winemakers skillfully combine the knowledge of old-world techniques with the innovation of new technologies to craft world-class wines. The majority of vineyards in the region are less than 15 years old. New plantings are positioned purposefully from north to south to make full use of the sun as it rises in the east and sets in the west. The green canopy of the vine acts as a giant solar panel that drives the fruit production. This positioning also makes full use of the natural air currents rolling south toward the Escarpment. Vines are also planted in specific densities determined by the fertility of the soil. The vine canopy is trained according to specific soil type in an effort to find the delicate balance between maximum yield and quality. Environmentally friendly canopy management techniques are used to stop mould, mildew and insect infestations before they take hold in the vineyard. All

of this is done to produce the best possible grape as it isn't possible to improve quality once the grape arrives at the winery door. Drastic improvements in mechanical harvesting allow grapes to be gently harvested 24 hours a day. The majority of vineyards in the area are independently owned by growers. As you drive through wine country, a residential home surrounded by vineyard is a common site. The grower most likely lives on the property, farms the land and sells the fruit to a nearby winery. Contracts can range from one to fifty years.

Production facilities in the region are among the world's most technologically advanced. Such large production facilities increase the quality of mass-produced wines and allow smaller facilities to craft premium wines that can compete internationally with any cool-climate wine region. Well-educated, bold, innovative winemakers are charged with the care of grapes that have been pampered since pruning in the early spring.

When white grapes are received at the winery, the stems are removed and the grapes are pumped into a press. The juice (now called "must") is moved to a tank or barrel where yeast is added and fermentation takes place. White wines are usually fermented "cool" at a temperature of 12 to 16 degrees Celsius (50 to 60 F) for a period of 7 to 10 days. This will ensure that the finished wine retains its fruity qualities. One of the important by-products of fermentation is alcohol. After fermentation, the wine is "racked," meaning it is moved to a new vessel, either stainless steel or oak barrel, to age for a potential period of 3 to 18 months. At this time, the wine may be filtered and aged in bottle before release to the public.

Red grapes also have their stems removed, but the must is pumped into an oak or stainless steel vessel for fermentation with its skins, seeds and pulp. The juice squeezed from a red grape is clear. What gives the red wines their colour and tannic, mouth-drying quality, comes from the juice contact ("maceration") with the skins for a period of 5 to 12 days. Reds are fermented "hot" at 22 to 30 degrees Celsius (71 to 86 F). After fermentation is complete, the juice is "racked" off the skins. At this time, the saturated skins are pressed and juice can be added to the finished wine and may be oak-aged before filtering and public release.

Canada's wine industry is most noted internationally for sweet and luscious icewine. Icewine was discovered in Germany in the late 1700s and is still produced there today. However, temperatures only reach cold enough levels there once or twice every decade to make this opulent dessert wine. Niagara winters balance precariously between being cold enough to produce world-class icewine and mild enough to grow vinifera grape vines. Icewine has been produced successfully every year in the Niagara region since 1983. The grapes are harvested frozen solid, at a minimum temperature of -8 degrees Celsius (17 F). Most growers like to see the temperature even colder than this, and will harvest from midnight till sunrise to avoid the danger of temperatures rising and stopping the production once it has begun. The grapes are pressed frozen solid in the winery, with the doors wide open to keep the grapes from thawing out. Any water left in the already-dehydrated grapes is frozen solid, resulting in a yield of only 10 percent of the grapes' volume. The juice is the consistency of honey when it comes out of the press. Icewine fermentation is extremely long. It is not uncommon for the fermentation to take several months, as the yeast must work hard on the sugary mixture.

All of these processes sound simple enough, but each step offers the winemaker many options, all of which will affect the wine's structure, intensity of flavour, aromas and overall quality. No two vintages are ever identical. Mother Nature changes the playing field from year to year.

NIAGARA'S PREDOMINANT
GRAPE VARIETIES

NIAGARA WINE COUNTRY IS STILL LARGELY UNDISCOVERED. THE REGION DOESN'T have the benefit of generations of quality wine production to dictate what grape varieties are best to grow in this climate. The attraction to participate in shaping the region's winemaking style is an exciting opportunity for any winemaker, and it's drawing talented winemakers from overseas. Cultivar experimentation is extreme, including more than 50 different grape varieties. Everything from Aligote to Zinfandel is planted in the region. However, there are some varieties that dominate the landscape.

WHITE GRAPE VARIETIES

CHARDONNAY is the most widely planted white vinifera grape variety in Niagara. When grown in cool climates, it retains its balance of acidity and apple and pear flavours. It's also relatively winter-hardy and ripens early, toward the end of September.

RIESLING offers value and consistency year after year. This variety was one of the first commercially planted vinifera grapes in the region. Highly versatile, this variety makes fantastic sparkling, dry, off-dry, semi-sweet and icewine styles. Its brilliant acidity is well matched by sweetness, leaving your palate refreshed, even when made into icewine.

GEWURZTRAMINER never disappoints, with its wild, over-the-top aromatics. Lychee nut and rosewater scents are hard to miss. The plant tends to grow dense foliage amongst pink-skinned fruit and requires significant management to combat potential mildew problems.

SAUVIGNON BLANC has become an increasingly popular planting, presenting excellent citrus, gooseberry, grassy and herbaceous notes when grown in a cool climate. It grows vigorously, even in poor soils, and ripens by the third week of October.

VIDAL is the most favoured variety for icewine, as it has large bunches of thick-skinned grapes, and maintains its acidity well into winter. It's often made into dry or off-dry inexpensive table wines that smell wonderfully of white blossoms.

Other varieties growing in popularity are **PINOT GRIS** (also called **PINOT GRIGIO**), **PINOT BLANC**, **VIOGNIER**, **CHENIN BLANC** and **SEMILLON**. These grapes are showing loads of promise, but are planted in micro-amounts.

RED GRAPE VARIETIES

CABERNET FRANC is the most widely planted red vinifera grape variety. Not only is it winter tolerant and high-yielding, but this grape variety also ripens a week or two before Cabernet Sauvignon. It is a natural match to this climate, producing medium to enormous full-bodied wines in hot growing years.

CABERNET SAUVIGNON represents everything that white wine lovers dislike about red wine. The small blue/black berries are harvested in late October or early November. This grape has the highest ratio of skin to juice. The result is a wine with huge tannin, acidity and ageability.

MERLOT has the least winter tolerance of all the region's big red varieties. It ripens in early October and, due to its thin skin, has lower tannin levels. Merlot is softer, fruitier and smoother than its big brothers.

PINOT NOIR is often referred to as "the heartbreak grape." This is a naturally low-yielding and finicky variety favoured in cool climates. The small, compact clusters are notoriously susceptible to bunch rot. At its best, Pinot makes some of the region's most elegant, well-balanced and most expensive table wines.

BACO NOIR and MARECHAL FOCH are hybrid grape varieties designed in the early 1900s. They make bigger, beefier, consistent red wines in cool climates. These wines are often made from older vines that produce low-yielding interesting fruit that, when combined with oak aging, can make spectacular wine. Don't knock it till you try it!

Other varieties showing promise and grown in small amounts include GAMAY, ZWEIGELT, and SYRAH (also called SHIRAZ). Experimentation continues with SANGIOVESE, NEBBIOLO and ZINFANDEL.

THE IMPORTANCE OF THE
VQA WINE COUNCIL
AND THE ONTARIO
GRAPE GROWERS'
MARKETING BOARD

WHAT IS THE VQA (VINTNERS QUALITY ALLIANCE)? ANY WINE-PRODUCING region in the world that takes itself seriously has a governing body that dictates quality assurance to protect consumers and the wine industry's reputation.

In 1988, an association of vintners formed the VQA to inform consumers of quality wines made exclusively from Ontario grapes. In 1999, the VQA Act was passed in the Ontario Legislature. Basically, when you purchase a VQA product, you can be assured that 100 percent of the grapes used to produce that wine were grown in one of three recognized Ontario viticultural areas. The wine must be made from approved grape varieties and must be produced from start to finish in Ontario. There are now legal consequences for non-compliance.

The Wine Council of Ontario is a non-profit trade organization that contributes to the marketing of Ontario wines. For example, they provide

the widely available wineroute map to the region. They also offer government relations support for its members. However, not all Niagara wineries choose to become members.

Established in 1947, the Ontario Grape Growers' Marketing Board is the official representative of more than 500 commercial grape growers in southern Ontario. This organization negotiates prices on behalf of the growers with the representative of the wineries, the Wine Council of Ontario. Growers in the area contract their fruit directly with wineries and these negotiations ensure that prices must be no less than the minimum agreed upon between the Wine Council and the Marketing Board. Bonuses can be provided to growers for higher-quality grapes with higher sugar levels, but this is negotiated between wineries and growers directly.

NIAGARA'S
WORLD-CLASS
WINERIES

ANGELS GATE WINERY

Turning south off King Street (the wine route) onto Mountainview Road, traveling up the Escarpment (fifty metres down the road from Thirty Bench Winery) you'll see a pale yellow mission-style building on your right-hand side, surrounded by vineyards. Enter through a black iron gate and follow the gravel road to Angels Gate Winery. The winery sits on a property once owned by the Congregation of Missionary Sisters of Christian Charity. After a stint as a mink farm in the 1950s and '60s the 23-acre property was abandoned until vines were planted in 1995. Seven years and thirteen investors later, the winery opened its doors in the early summer of 2002. Angels Gate's well-designed facility is dug into the hillside, with the barrel cellars, lab and fermentation tanks beneath the tasting boutique. This makes use of a naturally cool and moderate environment ideal for all winery operations, from pressing grapes to bottling the finished wine.

Angels Gate maintains two vineyards under the watchful eye of general manager Darryl Fields. These grapes are carefully crafted into superior wine by winemaker Natalie Spytkowsky. Working in the industry literally from the ground up, Natalie started her career pruning and hand-tying grape vines. In 1999, Natalie started her own independent wine lab and analysis company, providing services for over 40 wineries in Canada and the U.S. Although initially brought on board to consult for Angels Gate, she has happily made her position permanent. Natalie makes wine with focus. She attributes the character of her wine to her "less is more" philosophy. Minimizing fining and filtering procedures gives Natalie's wines more body, richness and intensity. Future production at Angels Gate will only reach 20,000 cases, allowing this team to focus on quality production in the years to come.

Natalie makes fantastic Riesling, offering a dry and off-dry "Sussreserve" (a German style of wine-making adding unfermented sweet juice to dry finished wine). You'll also find good value Old Vines Chardonnay here. There's also good Pinot made in small quantities, so pick up as much as you can, if there's any on the shelf.

4260 Mountainview Road
Beamsville ON L0R 1B1

T   905.563.3942
F   905.563.4127
W   www.angelsgatewinery.com

ANNUAL PRODUCTION
6,000 cases

ACREAGE
10 acres on site, 25 acres
5 kilometres from winery

WHEN TO VISIT
May to October
Daily 10–5, Sundays 11–5

November to April
Daily 11–5

LCBO AVAILABILITY
At winery only, delivery in Ontario

BIRCHWOOD ESTATE WINES

You may have passed by the Birchwood winery many times as you were speeding along the Queen Elizabeth Way (QEW) to and from Niagara Falls. Don't be fooled by the small size or proximity to the highway, there are some great wines to be tasted here.

The vineyard was planted by the Green family, who still live in the white, two-storey home on the property. The facility originally housed wines made under the Vine Court label. This site was also the home of Willow Heights Estates winery for four years, until a need to increase production moved them to their King Street location.

Opened in spring of 2000, this small facility sells wines actually made at Birchwood's sister winery, Lakeview Cellars. Production is under the watchful eye of winemaker Tom Green. While you're visiting, you might also recognize the second-label Salmon River wines from seeing them at the LCBO.

It's hard to beat the quality
of the Gewurztraminer
Riesling at its price point.
Give your beer a rest and
open a bottle next time
you bring home Thai food.
It's one of Birchwood's
biggest sellers.

4679 Cherry Avenue
Beamsville ON L0R 1B0

T   905.562.8463
F   905.562.6344
W www.birchwoodwines.com

ANNUAL PRODUCTION
10,000 cases

ACREAGE
10

WHEN TO VISIT
June to October
Daily 10–6, Sundays 11–5

November to April
Wednesday to Sunday 11–5

LCBO AVAILABILITY
Yes, Salmon River and Birchwood
widely available, some reserve
wines at winery only, delivery in
Ontario

CAROLINE CELLARS

Off the well-beaten track of Niagara Stone Road, located on Line 2 is Caroline Cellars. The winery is named after the family's paternal grandmother, who passed away years ago of cancer. Caroline, sister to the owner of Hernder Estate Winery, helped Rick and Frieda Lakeit finance the property over 30 years ago. The property was operated as a mixed fruit and vegetable farm, selling peppers, tomatoes and orchard fruit to locals and tourists alike.

Since then, the Lakeit family has expanded its holdings and manages vineyards on two farms. The family takes only a small percentage of the grapes produced for their own use. The majority of grapes are sold to Inniskillin Winery.

The building that houses the production area, lab, office, tasting room and special events loft was literally built by Rick Sr. and Jr. over an 18-month period and has been open since 2002. This is truly a family operation, with mother Frieda and twin daughters Justine and Stephanie managing the office, marketing and retail duties, while Rick Jr. manages the vineyard and assists Niagara College graduate and winemaker Jordan Harris.

All the winemaking is done in a 600-square-foot area where equipment has to be moved outside to make room for racking, filtering and bottling. Production is among the smallest in Niagara, with plans to push it up to 10,000 cases after expansion expected in 2005.

You'll love the approachability of these wines. They are fruit-forward in style, showing more berry fruit than barrel character. Rick Sr. is a solid advocate of value. He strongly believes that high prices are keeping Niagara wine off the kitchen tables of Canadian homes. If you have the chance to visit during one of the weekend BBQs, you're sure to leave feeling like you've had a visit to a leisurely family reunion.

Riesling is a favourite here, produced in an off-dry style, wonderful with jerk chicken or Indian curry. There's fantastic value in the Baco Noir and red Meritage. The Vidal and Cabernet Franc icewine is a steal, at half the price of some of the competition. It's difficult to beat the value of these wines. Buy in large quantities, drink daily and order more!

1028 Line 2
N.O.T.L. ON L0S 1J0

T   905.468.8814
F   905.468.4042
W www.lakeitfarms.com

ANNUAL PRODUCTION
2,500 cases

ACREAGE
40

WHEN TO VISIT
Daily 10–6
Sunday 11–6

LCBO AVAILABILITY
None, delivery in Ontario

CAVE SPRING CELLARS

Driving east through the Jordan Valley, you'll cross Twenty Mile Creek and quickly find Main Street to your left. If you miss this turn, take 19th street and turn left down Wismer and you'll find yourself in Jordan Village, home to some of Niagara West's best shopping and eateries. You'll also find Cave Spring Cellars in the centre of this pretty tree-lined street.

Angelo Pavan has been making distinctive wines since 1986 in the old Jordan Wines facility, originally built in 1871. Leonard Pennachetti teamed up with Angelo in the early 1980s and their first vintage produced a few hundred cases of Riesling. Over the next decade, vineyard holdings were dramatically increased and extensive work undertaken to realize the vision of what is now Jordan Village.

The winery's proprietary vineyards are several kilometres east of the facility, on some of the region's best vine-growing land. The original 12-acre parcel was purchased in 1973 by John Pennachetti. A unique feature of the Cave Spring vineyard is the increased density of the vines. At two to three times the volume of vines per acre than the rest of the region's, the plants struggle to force their roots deep into the subsoil hunting for moisture and nutrients. The results are in the glass.

Reserve Riesling is absolutely fantastic here, and undervalued. Age for three to seven years and serve with Scottish smoked salmon with red onion. Angelo's Gamay is consistently good, serving as a regional benchmark for this grape varietal. Great with summertime grilled fish or pork tenderloin.

3836 Main Street
Jordan ON L0R 1S0

T 905.562.3581
F 905.562.3232
W www.cavespringcellars.com

ANNUAL PRODUCTION
60,000 cases

ACREAGE
130

WHEN TO VISIT
May to October
Daily 10–6, Sunday 11–6
November to April
Daily 10–5, Sunday 11–5

LCBO AVAILABILITY
Yes, widely available across Canada, several U.S. states, with some Reserve CSV wines available at the winery only, delivery in Ontario

CHATEAU DES CHARMES ESTATE WINERY

Driving along York Road north of the QEW, it is impossible to miss a huge stone mansion in the centre of an expansive vineyard. The building was constructed in 1993 by the Bosc family. Paul and Andrée Bosc immigrated to Canada from France in the 1960s. Paul Bosc received his education from the University of Bourgogne in Dijon and is a fifth-generation grape grower. The young family moved to Niagara from Montreal where Paul was the winemaker at Château-Gai for 15 years before founding Château Des Charmes in 1978.

As you drive past the stately grounds, you will notice numerous windmills strategically positioned amongst the vines. Because of the property's distance to the moderating effect of the lake, these specially-designed windmills were installed to pull warm air above the vineyard and push it in and amongst the vines. This can raise the temperature in the vineyard to 4 to 5 degrees Celsius (39 to 41 F) on the coldest nights of winter and can also prevent damaging frost from settling on the vines in early spring and mid-fall.

The winery facilities are huge and can accommodate weddings with hundreds of guests. Paul makes wines now with his son Pierre-Jean. Mother Andrée, son Paul-André and wife Michele manage the facility's operations and marketing. Still a family enterprise, this winery has not lost sight of its roots. Paul is heavily invested in research of specific clones of grapevines that will be best suited to Niagara's mesoclimate.

These top-quality wines are separated into the St. David's Bench and Paul Bosc Estate vineyards. The Gamay Droit is one of my favourites. Established in 1982, this particular clone grows in an upright ("droit") manner in the vineyard and produces fantastic fruit. This is one of the region's best. The Viognier is made in a medium-bodied fruity style. All of the big reds have good weight and intensity, representing good value.

1025 York Road
N.O.T.L. ON L0S 1S0

T 905.262.4219
F 905.262.5548
W www.chateaudescharmes.com

ANNUAL PRODUCTION
100,000 cases

ACREAGE
280

WHEN TO VISIT
Daily 10–6

LCBO AVAILABILITY
Yes, limited selections at winery only, delivery in Ontario

COYOTE'S RUN ESTATE WINERY

Several hundred metres north of Queenston Road, on Concession 5, you'll discover the entrance to Coyote's Run winery on the west side of the road. A long thin drive leads you up to the metal-clad winery that sits in the middle of the proprietary vineyard. The winery was named after the movements of the local wild canines.

The project has been developed by partners Jeff Aubry and Steve Murzda. They have attracted the help of long-time Inniskillin winemaker David Sheppard, who is sourcing grapes from both on-site vineyards and Steve Murzda's property a few kilometres toward St. David's. Strict vineyard control allows this team complete dedication to fruit quality. The same rows are harvested several times, as bunches are individually picked when they have reached optimal ripeness. This is time-consuming and costly, but the rewards are evident in the quality of the finished wines.

The facility is uncomplicated, designed for a maximum 10,000-case production. David utilizes French and Hungarian oak aging in the small but functional cellar. If you like well-balanced, structured wines, this is your stop.

The Chardonnay is brilliant here. You may appreciate the reserved and controlled use of oak. The reserve Pinot Noir is a weighty, intense monster, a killer style that's atypical for Niagara. Serve with pan-seared duck breast and polenta. David, keep the beefy Pinot coming, we love it!

485 Concession 5 Road
N.O.T.L. ON L0S 1J0

T   905.682.8310
     1.877.269.6833 (toll free)
F   905.682.1166
W www.coyotesrunwinery.com

ANNUAL PRODUCTION
2,500 cases

ACREAGE
60

WHEN TO VISIT
May to October
Daily 11–6

November to April
Thursday to Monday 11–5

LCBO AVAILABILITY
At winery only, delivery in Ontario

CREEKSIDE ESTATE WINERY

Driving along what feels like a remote stretch of Fourth Avenue on the western outskirts of St. Catharines, you'll find the entrance to Creekside Estate Winery at the crest of a small hill, east of Thirteenth Street. A winding driveway leads you to a small wood-clad tasting room next to an expansive covered deck where tasty grilled foods are offered on the weekend by Chef David Paquet from early summer through fall.

Creekside has been owned by Peter and Laura McCain-Jensen since 1998. After an inspirational visit to California, the couple purchased the small-production V.P. Cellars. The production area and underground cellar were soon built to expand the volume and portfolio.

Laura and Peter have enlisted Rob Power and Craig McDonald to head up this hard-working winemaking team. To their credit, I have a tough time finding a wine at Creekside I don't like. Grapes are sourced from the on-site vineyard as well as the Paragon Vineyards along the St. David's Bench in Niagara-on-the-Lake, and from contracted local growers.

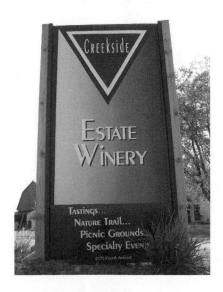

You can't leave Niagara without sampling the Sauvignon Blanc. The Laura's Blend offers consistent southern-hemisphere style, difficult to achieve with Niagara's short, cool growing season. The Signature series Shiraz is loaded with character and intense fruit, and priced to match. Serve with juicy grilled meats to pair with the wine's intensity.

2170 Fourth Avenue
Jordan Station ON L0R 1S0

T   905.562.0035
    1.877.262.9463 (toll free)
F   905.562.5493
W   www.creeksideestatewinery.com

ANNUAL PRODUCTION
25,000 cases

ACREAGE
13

WHEN TO VISIT
May to October
Daily 10–6

November to April
Daily 11–5

LCBO AVAILABILITY
At winery only, delivery in Ontario

CROWN BENCH ESTATES WINERY

At the southern end of Aberdeen Road, just metres away from the Bruce Trail, you will find Crown Bench Estates. Situated on a 30-acre vineyard toward the top of the Niagara Escarpment, the property boasts a block of 30-year-old Chardonnay. The winery is located inside a large brick home at the south end of the property.

After 35 years of amateur winemaking and years of selling fruit to nearby Thirty Bench Winery, Peter Kocsis and Liva Sipos opened their doors in 1999. High-quality, low-production wines are the focus of this small winery that concentrates on diligent vineyard management. Peter's philosophy is that great wines aren't made, they're grown. Liva, who cares for the property's vineyards, was named Grape King in 2004, an award for Ontario's best vineyard.

Peter's focus is rich Chardonnay and bold Bordeaux-style reds. He has also created some unique dessert wines, including late-harvested botrytis-affected Chardonnay, made in a similar style to the dessert wines of Sauterne. Botrytis is a specific mold that dehydrates the grape to increase sugar levels and flavour intensity. Current production is small and will most likely remain that way, as Peter wants to keep his focus on quality.

Peter's Reserve Chardonnay is big, rich and creamy. Try this weighty, serious wine with grilled cedar-planked salmon. His Vintners Reserve Cabernet Franc is bold and powerful, my favourite of all his big reds. If you can wait, it will benefit from time in your cellar.

3850 Aberdeen Road
Beamsville ON L0R 1B7

T 905.563.3959
    1.888.537.6192 (toll free)
F 905.563.3441
W www.crownbenchestates.com

ANNUAL PRODUCTION
5,000 cases

ACREAGE
30

WHEN TO VISIT
Daily 10–5

LCBO AVAILABILITY
At winery only, delivery in Ontario

DANIEL LENKO ESTATE WINERY

The rumours you may have heard about Daniel Lenko winery are true. Yes, the total production is sold from the family farmhouse kitchen. Yes, mother Helen Lenko's hospitality is genuine and magical, accompanied with a warm piece of apple pie, oatmeal cookie or heavenly spice cake. And yes, the property boasts some of Canada's oldest vines.

When on King Street, near the western edge of Beamsville, look for a small sign marked "open" or "closed" on the railing to the kitchen entrance of the raised brick bungalow. Purchased in 1947, the property served as a mixed fruit farm until 1958, when Daniel's father Bill planted a small block of Chardonnay. Merlot and Cabernet Sauvignon soon followed. As you drive up to the entrance to the property on King Street, you can see how thick and dark the vines are. Many of Niagara's pioneering wineries sourced grapes from this vineyard. Daniel took over the operation from his father in the late '90s, opening in 2000 with the 1999 vintage. Enlisting the help of local wine legend Jim Warren proved to be a great move to ensure a high-quality finished wine, now eagerly anticipated by fans near and far.

Wines are only available for sale from February through mid-summer, when the inventory gets sold out! Enjoy your time at the kitchen table and, when you're leaving with a case of wine, be sure to take home some of Helen's apricot jam. It's the best.

SOMMELIER'S PICKS

The "Old Vines" Merlot is popular and may be available only by the case. The "Old Vines" Chardonnay is produced in both French and American oak; this represents a great comparative tasting. Buy as much as possible of the Viognier. This is one of the region's cult wines, and even on the off-chance you don't like it, you could ransom it off on the Internet for a small fortune. If you order by the case to your home, don't be surprised to see Daniel pull up in his retrofitted Cadillac/delivery car rumoured to hold over 50 cases!

5246 Regional Road 81
Beamsville ON L0R 1B3

T 905.563.7756
F 905.563.3317
W www.daniellenko.com

ANNUAL PRODUCTION
5,000 cases

ACREAGE
30

WHEN TO VISIT
February to mid-summer
Saturday and Sunday 12–5

Get on the email list!

LCBO AVAILABILITY
At winery only, delivery in Ontario

DE SOUSA WINE CELLARS

The winding drive south up Quarry Road feels somewhat remote as you pass by ivy-covered Victorian brick homes and manicured vineyards. As you near the top of the Escarpment, you'll find De Sousa Wine Cellars. The bodega-style winery is noticeably European. The established, well-manicured grounds and clay wine cups give this winery distinct old-world charm. The original 22-acre vineyard was established here in 1979. Years later, the family acquired the adjacent property to expand on the production.

John De Sousa has taken the winemaking over from his father, John Sr., who passed away in 1997. John Sr. immigrated to Canada from Portugal in 1961, and much of this winery's production is still sold to the Portuguese communities in the Toronto area. Andre Lipinski has been the consulting winemaker here since the 2001 vintage, crafting all the Reserve series wines.

The Sauvignon Blanc here is wonderfully herbaceous and grassy. Pair with grilled asparagus and goat cheese dishes. All the reds have a rustic old-world charm to them. The Cabernet Franc reserve has delightful dusty tannins. Enjoy with rich, gamey meats.

3753 Quarry Road
Beamsville ON L0R 1B0

T 905.563.7269
F 905.338.9404
W www.desousawines.com

ANNUAL PRODUCTION
20,000 cases

ACREAGE
85

WHEN TO VISIT
May to October
Daily 10:30–5:30

November to April
weekends only 10:30–5

LCBO AVAILABILITY
At winery only, second location in Toronto, delivery in Ontario

DOMAINE VAGNERS

If you think you've visited every established winery in the region, you might be surprised to discover this one. If you're not easily discouraged, you'll hunt for its small, ivy-covered white and green street sign marked "1973" on Four Mile Creek Road, just north of East/West Line. Turn into the two-lane gravel driveway, and as you approach the old red barn you will see a small hand-drawn sign on the right side of the doorway marked Domaine Vagners. Feel free to park on the grass, as there is no official parking lot.

Martin Vagners moved his family to the property from Etobicoke after planting the small vineyard in 1990. Martin's first vintage was released in 1993. Small quantity and high quality has always been the focus of his efforts. Any finished wines that Martin isn't completely satisfied with are simply not available for purchase. A small expansion on the barn was added in 2004 to accommodate a barrel cellar and larger tasting area. However, Martin will be the first to tell you that production isn't increasing now, or ever. Small is good.

The Pinot Noir is good, and undervalued, rustic and Burgundian in style with firm tannin and ample fruit. The Rieslings are Alsatian in style, fruity, with excellent minerality and acidity. All of these wines are made in micro-amounts. Support the region's smallest winery and take home a bottle or twelve.

1973 Four Mile Creek Road R.R. 3
N.O.T.L. ON L0S 1J0

T 905.468.7296
W Not yet

ANNUAL PRODUCTION
In 2003, 1,000 litres

ACREAGE
5

WHEN TO VISIT
Year round
Saturdays only 11–3
I'd recommend phoning ahead.

LCBO AVAILABILITY
At winery only

EASTDELL ESTATE WINERY

Driving south up Mountainview Road from King Street, turn left at Locust Lane and follow signs to EastDell Estates Winery. The property is truly welcoming, with views of Lake Ontario and a five-kilometre self-guidable walking trail past estate vineyards, lush wooded areas and picturesque ponds. The property houses the Bench Bistro, featuring fresh seasonal flavours, as well as the Heron's Nest, a private retreat for couples on the edge of EastDell pond.

The winery was founded in 1999 by entrepreneur Susan O'Dell and partner Michael East. Grapes are sourced from 42 planted acres on two properties along the Bench. After a turbulent past, the future is certainly rosy for this growing wine company. Talented winemaker Jason James and famed consultant Jim Warren are heading up the winemaking team. In the spring of 2004, the company acquired Thomas & Vaughan Winery on King Street. This is indeed a sign of great things to come for this growing wine company.

Unoaked Chardonnay leads the pack here. The fresh, fun Summer Rosé is always a good dinner party starter on a patio. The Cuvee Brut sparkling is a delicious deal under $20, the perfect brunch wine!

4041 Locust Lane
Beamsville ON L0R 1B2

T 905.563.9463
F 905.563.1241
W www.eastdell.com

ANNUAL PRODUCTION
17,000 cases

ACREAGE
62

WHEN TO VISIT
Daily 9–8
Closed Mondays in the winter

LCBO AVAILABILITY
Yes, some products at winery only, delivery in Ontario

FEATHERSTONE ESTATE WINERY

Don't be surprised if you haven't heard of Featherstone Estate Winery. One of the area's best kept secrets, Featherstone is nestled amongst the vines on Victoria Avenue south of King Street in an 1830s farmhouse. Views from Niagara's largest verandah, overlooking vineyards to Lake Ontario, make this a great stop for a summer weekend luncheon.

In 1998, David Johnson and Louise Engel purchased the vineyard, long before selling their well-established Guelph Gourmet Poultry Market. This hard-working couple would commute on days off to tend to the vineyard, install new grape varietals and renovate what is now the winery and retail shop.

Their dedication and commitment does not stop there. David is absolutely meticulous in his vineyard maintenance. The property is herbicide-free, using natural predators and pheromone traps to control harmful insects. Recycled wood chips are placed around vines to control weeds and conserve moisture during drought months.

In 2003, David was crowned Grape King by the Ontario Grape Growers' Marketing Board. David focuses on producing wine in small batches from grapes produced exclusively on their property. The result is wines not only of high quality but fantastic character as well. Louise's warmth, hospitality and friendly knowledge of wine make a visit to this winery a real treat for the enthusiast and novice alike. If timing permits, ask her about the Harris hawk she trained to patrol the vineyard against hungry birds stealing sweet grapes at harvest time.

The future production of wine at Featherstone will only reach 6,000 cases. Such micro-production allows this dynamic duo to control all aspects of their operation. These wines are truly handcrafted.

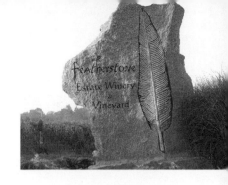

SOMMELIER'S PICKS

Dave makes a great Gewurztraminer. Not your average Niagara "G" wine, this friendly sipper has a classic ginger and rose-petal quality. This is a great wine to get a dinner party rolling. Do your best to get some of Dave's Gamay. His is one of the region's finest examples of this grape varietal, and one he is proud of, with loads of berry fruit balanced with firm tannins and welcoming acidity. Try this food-accessible wine slightly chilled, with grilled fish.

3678 Victoria Avenue
Vineland ON L0R 2C0

T 905.562.1949
F 905.562.3989
W www.featherstonewinery.ca

ANNUAL PRODUCTION
3,500 cases

ACREAGE
23

WHEN TO VISIT
April to December
Friday to Monday 11–6

LCBO AVAILABILITY
At winery only, delivery in Ontario

FIELDING ESTATE WINERY

Driving south up the Escarpment on Mountainview Road, you will see Fielding Estate Winery at the corner of Locust Lane. The winery opened in the spring of 2005. Ken and Marg Fielding have enlisted the help of consulting winemaker Andrzej Lipinski. With the help of their son Curtis as assistant winemaker, small-batch, high-quality wines are highly anticipated from this boutique facility. Sleek architecture, the finest technology and a hands-on attitude to vineyard management are the mantra of this new winery.

On-site and lakeshore vineyards are cared for by local vineyard manager Duarte Oliveira, ensuring only the best, premium, low-yielding fruit makes its way to the winery door for processing. Syrah and Pinot Noir will be the focus here, with smaller amounts of Chardonnay, Riesling and Pinot Gris. The winery has been built to accommodate a maximum of 15,000 cases.

Wines were unavailable for tasting at the time of writing. The winery will release a Chardonnay and Cabernet-Merlot upon opening.

4020 Locust Lane
Beamsville ON L0R 1B2

T 905.327.6202
W www.fieldingwines.com

ANNUAL PRODUCTION
2002 vintage, 400 cases

ACREAGE
30

WHEN TO VISIT
May to October
Daily 11–5

November to April
Call or email ahead.

LCBO AVAILABILITY
At winery only, delivery in Ontario

FLAT ROCK CELLARS

Driving along Seventh Avenue between 19th and 21st Streets, you'll see a small Inuit Inukshuk sculpture, marked Flat Rock Cellars, standing a few feet off the ground on the north side of the road. As you approach the facility, you'll notice two distinct six-sided glass, steel and concrete buildings connected by a glass-enclosed bridge.

The right-hand side houses the tasting bar and private-function room. Floor-to-ceiling windows and elevated architecture allow for a spectacular view over the property and out to Lake Ontario.

The left-hand building houses an ingenious production facility designed to work with gravity and geothermal heating and cooling. Numerous small open-top fermentation tanks allow winemaker Darryl Brooker to craft small batches of his premium wine. Darryl is an Australian-trained viticulturalist with extensive winemaking experience in the Barossa Valley and New Zealand.

The winery has been open since August of 2004 and is devoted to small production of cool-climate favourites, Riesling, Chardonnay and Pinot Noir. The production will only reach 15,000 cases. Fruit is sourced exclusively from the estate property and Darryl is experimenting with different clones in each grape variety in an effort to discover superior fruit on this particular vineyard site. One thing you're certain to notice is the closure system of the bottles. One hundred percent of the production is sealed with screw caps (brand name Stelvin). Flat Rock is the first winery in Niagara to devote its entire production to the cleanest bottle-topper available to the wine industry.

SOMMELIER'S PICKS

The Rieslings are fresh,
crisp and clean. Try the
"Nadja's Vineyard"
Riesling. It has a wonderful minerality with a tart,
bracing and lingering finish.
The Chardonnay is grace-
ful and well designed in
Burgundian style with
good acidity and bright
fruity flavours with a
vanilla and toffee bouquet.
Pinot Noir will be the main
focus of production here.

2727 7th Avenue
Jordan ON L0R 1S0

T 905.562.8994
F 905.562.9162
W www.flatrockcellars.com

ANNUAL PRODUCTION
2,500 cases

ACREAGE
70

WHEN TO VISIT
May to October
Daily 10–6

November to April
Saturday and Sunday 10–6

LCBO AVAILABILITY
At winery only, delivery in Ontario

FROGPOND FARM

Do you buy "organic" food? Welcome to the province's only certified organic winery. A few hundred metres south of Marynissen Estates Winery on Concession 1, you'll stumble across Larkin Road. A few hundred feet down, on the south side of the road, follow the gravel lane to a large red barn and outbuildings.

The vineyards were planted in 1996, and the first vintage was produced in 2001. Jens Gemmrich and Heike Koch use no fungicides, pesticides, herbicides or chemical-based fertilizers to manage their vineyards. Vigorous and labour-intensive canopy management techniques are employed to keep potential mould and insect problems at bay. This is a holistic approach to farming that must be earned. The National Standard of Canada for Organic Agriculture is the governing body that inspects, audits and certifies products deemed organic.

Those of you who suffer from headaches after drinking red wines may want to give the Cabernet-Merlot a try. The wine industry commonly adds sulfur dioxide (Sulfites, SO_2) to wine and barrels to sterilize and control microbial growth, preserving fruit flavours. The organic designation allows for only naturally-occurring sulfates produced by fermenting yeast in the wine. It's impossible for wine to be free of sulfur. However, organic wines contain a fraction of the sulfur found in non-organic wines. If sulfites are the culprit of your thumping head after consumption, give organic a try—it may permit you to enjoy red wine again.

Only two wines were available for tasting at the time of writing. The Riesling is big in body and mineral flavours. The Cabernet-Merlot is a solid wine with earthy, dark fruit flavours. All bottles are sold in 500 ml format.

1385 Larkin Road R.R. 6
N.O.T.L. ON L0S 1J0

T 905.468.1079
F 905.468.5665
W www.frogpondfarm.ca

ANNUAL PRODUCTION
2,500 cases

ACREAGE
10

WHEN TO VISIT
Year Round
Tuesday to Saturday 1–5

LCBO AVAILABILITY
At winery only, delivery in Ontario

HARBOUR ESTATES WINERY

On the west side of Jordan Road, across from Paul's Garage, you'll notice a small sign directing you past a residential home to Harbour Estates Winery. Although you're not able to see it from the tasting room, the property sits on 1,800 feet of waterfront on Jordan Harbour. The water next to this vineyard site moderates the vineyard in all seasons.

The facility is owned and operated by the Mowat family. Fraser and Darlene Mowat originally purchased the property for orchard, but from 1997 to 2002 the property was converted to exclusively red-grape varietals. White grapes are sourced from other growers. Fourth-generation farmer Ken Mowat is one of the youngest winemakers in the region.

Currently, wines are made in the large building behind the tasting area; however, the family is considering new construction on the waterfront of the property to accommodate an expanding portfolio. Numerous events are held at this winery year round, from grape-stomping competitions to food and music festivals and falconry demonstrations.

What you'll love about these wines is their approachability and price point. Ken designs the wines for consumption upon release. The Rieslings are delicious and the Cabernet and blends are a great, fruit forward buy under $20.

4362 Jordan Road
Jordan Station ON L0R 1S0

T   905.562.6279
F   905.562.3829
W www.hewwine.com

ANNUAL PRODUCTION
15,000 cases

ACREAGE
30

WHEN TO VISIT
June to October
Daily 10–6

November to May
Daily 12–5

LCBO AVAILABILITY
At winery only, delivery in Ontario

HARVEST ESTATE WINES

Harvest Estate Wines is located on the western edge of St. Catharines on Eighth Avenue, attached to the Harvest Barn fresh food market. Along with your purchase of baked seasonal pies, you can sample wines made by consultant Ray Cornell, winemaker at Hernder Estate Wines.

The grapes are sourced primarily from proprietary vineyards planted in 2002 on-site and from well-established nearby properties. The small production facility is located a few thousand feet from the retail store. Tours can be arranged with advance notice. The wines are extremely approachable in flavour and price point.

The Rieslings are fresh and clean, with long, satisfying flavours. The Chardonnay is inexpensive, loaded with tropical fruit. The Baco Noir is good, a steal under $10. Pair with BBQ burgers and friends.

1607 8th Avenue
St. Catharines ON L2R 6P7

T 905.682.0080
F 905.682.0640
W www.harvestwines.com

ANNUAL PRODUCTION
4,000 cases

ACREAGE
10

WHEN TO VISIT
Daily 10–6

LCBO AVAILABILITY
Yes, some wines at winery only, delivery in Ontario

HENRY OF PELHAM
FAMILY ESTATE WINERY

On the southwestern edge of St. Catharines, a few hundred metres from the road entrance to Hernder, you'll find Henry of Pelham Family Estate Winery, located on the corner of Fifth Street and Pelham Road. With a new housing development in the distance it is hard to imagine this was once the site of an inn/tavern at the crossroads of three rural townships.

More than 160 years later, descendants of the original owner, Paul, Daniel and Matt Speck, operate this well-known winery with winemaker Ron Giesbrecht. In 1984, the then-teenaged brothers helped their father plant the property with vinifera varieties. In 1987, the winery was established, and in 1990 Ron was brought on board as part of the team. Since that time production has grown exponentially. Wind machines have been added to protect vines from winter damage, and the Coach House Café serves up rustic local fare May through October. Both the facility and wines have kept a crafted and homey feel to them. The Henry of Pelham team, never shy of innovation, has released the first VQA-approved screw-cap bottle. They have also found new avenues to market their wines on domestic and international airlines.

I have yet to find a wine here that I don't like. Riesling and Pinot Noir really stand out. Also, perhaps the most infamous wine in the region, Baco Noir, has really been put on the map by Henry of Pelham. I dare those skeptics who turn their noses up at hybrid grape varieties to sample the Reserve Baco. The grapes are cropped under three tons an acre. The 20+ year-old plants produce intense fruit that lends itself to extended American oak aging. Prepare to be converted! The Catharine

1469 Pelham Road
St. Catharines ON L2R 6P7

T   905.684.8423
      1.877.735.4267 (toll free)
F   905.684.8444
W   www.henryofpelham.com

ANNUAL PRODUCTION
80,000 cases

ACREAGE
150

WHEN TO VISIT
May to October
Daily 10–6

November to April
Daily 10–5

LCBO AVAILABILITY
Yes, some reserves released to the Vintages catalogue, some reserve wines at winery only

Sparkling Rosé is one of the area's best bottles of bubbles.

HERNDER ESTATE WINERY

Just a few hundred metres north of Henry of Pelham Winery, on Fifth Street, you'll see a green and white sign directing you down Eighth Avenue to Hernder Estate Winery. As you approach the winery you'll notice the romantic setting. This is one of the wedding destinations in Niagara, with a pond, covered bridge and Victorian barn that can accommodate 500 guests.

In 1939, Gottfried Hernder immigrated to Canada from Germany and eventually settled in St. Catharines. By the early 1970s, Jack Hernder was farming mixed fruit on a 60-acre parcel in Niagara-on-the-Lake. During the 1980s, the family expanded their holdings significantly and now have one of the largest privately-owned vineyards in the region. The winery site and signature 1867 barn were bought in 1987 by Fred Hernder, and the winery produced its first vintage in 1991. Ray Cornell is the winemaker here and at the sister winery, Harvest Estate Wines.

Ray is one of the region's Riesling kings, offering consistent quality and value in this varietal. At Hernder, Gewurztraminer is made in smaller production in a rich "boudoir" style. Both Cabernet Franc and Meritage from the 2002 vintage are massive and weighty, needing some time in your cellar, or several hours in a decanter before your guests arrive for dinner.

1607 8th Avenue
St. Catharines ON L2R 6P7

T 905.684.3300
F 905.684.3303
W www.hernder.com

ANNUAL PRODUCTION
45,000 cases

ACREAGE
500

WHEN TO VISIT
Daily 10–5

July to September
Daily 10–5
Saturdays 10–8

LCBO AVAILABILITY
Yes, some product at winery only, delivery in Ontario

HILLEBRAND ESTATES WINERY

The first winery you'll come across on Niagara Stone Road (Highway 55), heading northeast toward the old town of Niagara-on-the-Lake, is Hillebrand Estates Winery. The property and winery, established in 1979 under the name Newark Winery by Dr. Joseph Pohorly, was renamed Hillebrand in 1983, and sold in 1985 to the Swiss company, Underburg. Andres Wines purchased the winery in 1994 and has significantly increased production, distributing through their many retail outlets and online delivery service. The property is romantic and sprawling, with production, retail and restaurant located in separate buildings.

Grapes are sourced from proprietary vineyards and local growers, including the Huebel and Glenlake vineyards that make Hillebrand's flagship wines. The winemaking production area has extensive barrel cellars where the traditional-method Trius Brut Sparkling wine is aged. Winemaker J.L. Groux joined the winery in 1989. This makes him a seasoned veteran in the region. J.L. is originally from the Loire Valley and studied winemaking in both Bordeaux and Burgundy. More focus on vineyard grape conditions and less time handling the wine in production give J.L.'s wines a certain finesse and distinctive character that have earned them countless awards.

The Trius series are all good; my favourite is the Chardonnay. The sparkling has a wonderful toasted, yeasty, biscuity quality at a fraction of the cost of Champagne. Serve with malpeque oysters on Valentine's Day!

1249 Niagara Stone Road
N.O.T.L. ON L0S 1J0

T 905.468.7123
   1.800.582.8412 (toll free)
F 905.468.4789
W www.hillebrand.com

ANNUAL PRODUCTION
250,000 cases

ACREAGE
83

WHEN TO VISIT
Daily 10–6

LCBO AVAILABILITY
Yes, 100+ stores across Ontario,
delivery in Ontario

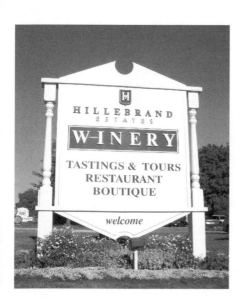

INNISKILLIN WINES

Just south of Reif Estates Winery on the Niagara Parkway, you'll see a black and gold sign marked Inniskillin, directing you west, down Line 3. A few hundred metres down Line 3, turn left into the entrance, past the vineyards and sprawling wine facility and you'll end up in front of the winery's signature Brae Burn Barn. This building houses the retail boutique and tasting bar and is rumoured to be the design of Frank Lloyd Wright. This winery is steeped in Niagara wine history. In the summer of 1975, partners Donald Ziraldo and Karl Kaiser were granted the first winery licence to be issued in over 45 years by the Ontario government. What followed from their first vintages of hybrid-based wines was extensive planting of vinifera. In 1991, Inniskillin brought the first international attention to Niagara as a quality wine-producing region with a gold award at Vinexpo in Bordeaux.

Donald Ziraldo has tirelessly promoted Canadian wine over the decades, literally around the world. He has also helped to raise millions for expansion at Niagara College and Brock University and is a huge supporter of Canada's Olympic athletes. Founder Karl Kaiser now makes wine with Philip Dowell, who oversees quality production in this large-volume facility. Fruit is sourced from the estate and nearby vineyards, many of which are a stone's throw from the winery.

Inniskillin has the region's best self-guided tour. Information stations lead you through vineyard and winery at your own pace. Don't be surprised to see one of the founders at the winery; they love what they do and it shows in the excellence of their wines.

Icewine is this winery's leading product around the planet. For wine enthusiasts who have everything in their cellar, sparkling icewine is something to pick up here. The Founders Reserve Chardonnay is one of the region's best. The Single Vineyard Pinot Noir from the Klose property is consistently fantastic and expensive.

S.R. 66 R.R. 1 Niagara Parkway
N.O.T.L. ON L0R 1J0

T 905.468.2187
   1.888.466.4754 (toll free)
F 905.468.5355
W www.inniskillin.com

ANNUAL PRODUCTION
120,000 cases

ACREAGE
130

WHEN TO VISIT
May to October
Daily 10–6

November to April
Daily 10–5

LCBO AVAILABILITY
Yes, and widely available across Canada, U.S., Asia and some European countries, delivery in Ontario

JACKSON-TRIGGS NIAGARA ESTATE WINERY

There's little doubt in my mind that if you live in Canada you've heard of, bought or consumed a bottle of Jackson-Triggs wine. In 1989, the Labatt brewing company was looking to part with its Canadian wine interests. Former employees Donald Triggs and Allan Jackson negotiated a buyout. Developments of the Jackson-Triggs brand quickly led to a rapid expansion of the business. Fifteen years later, the publicly-traded parent company, Vincor, has acquired wine companies in Australia, New Zealand, California, Washington and British Columbia.

The Niagara Estate facility was built in 2001 to make J-T's flagship premium VQA wines, and has been designed with a tour in mind. The facility houses state-of-the-art technology with the capacity for nearly one million litres of wine. The building is surprisingly environmentally friendly. Instead of central air conditioning, air is purposefully circulated around the cooled stainless steel tanks to moderate the temperature. Toronto architects K.P.M.B. are also responsible for the uniquely "Niagara" design. Wine and food events, progressive meals through the winery and open-air amphitheatre musical performances are scheduled regularly throughout the year.

Jackson-Triggs is truly in the winemaking business. For all the hundreds of thousands of cases of wine the company produces, they own only a small percentage of land. Fruit is purchased through local growers via long-and short-term leases. Harvested fruit is in the capable hands of winemaker Tom Seaver and his assistant Kristine Casey. Tom's background in wine theory and practice is extensive, and he and his team produce modern wine in larger volumes while keeping a full-flavoured feel to them. Not an easy task when hundreds of tons of fruit are received at the winery gate each fall.

SOMMELIER'S PICKS

It's rumoured that co-founder Allan Jackson is one of the world's greatest fans of Gewurztraminer. It shows in the quality expression of this varietal, and it's difficult to beat the price point. If you're a Champagne fan, you'll love the Methode Classique sparkling. Bracing acidity and biscuity vanilla notes make this wine a steal! Look for the Delaine Single Vineyard series. These are wines with distinct character made from Donald and Elaine Triggs' private vineyard. The Grand Reserve "gold label" big reds are half the cost of some of the competition's reserve wines.

2145 R.R. 55
N.O.T.L. ON L0S 1J0
T 905.468.4637
   1.866.589.4637 (toll free)
F 905.468.4673
W www.jacksontriggswinery.com

ANNUAL PRODUCTION
100,000 cases

ACREAGE
11

WHEN TO VISIT
Daily 10–6

LCBO AVAILABILITY
Although J-T wines are well represented throughout Canada, some of the wines produced at this facility are available only at this winery. Enquire about your favourites

JOSEPH'S ESTATE WINES

As you approach East/West Line driving north on Niagara Stone Road, you'll find a burgundy and white sign marked "Joseph's" on the east side of the road. The long paved driveway takes you up to a stone-clad building. The interior of the tasting area is warm and homey. A long, large, three-sided tasting bar is loaded with great wines to sample. The winery is named after Dr. Joseph Pohorly, truly one of the industry's pioneers. Born near Vineland, Joseph grew up on the family fruit farm and went on to become a teacher, later an engineer, before plunging into the wine business. Joseph started Newark winery in the late 1970s and eventually sold the winery now known as Hillebrand. Joseph made the winery's first icewine in 1983.

In 1992, the current winery location was purchased. This is a family business, with Joseph's daughter Caroline running the operation. Joseph can often be seen at the winery when not travelling to promote his products. In 2003, a 10,000-square-foot building was constructed to accommodate expanding production. The portfolio is large, including some interesting fruit wines.

Pinot Gris is consistently good here; Joseph feels that the vineyard soil is well suited to this grape variety. The Reserve Merlot is delicious, with a non-reserve price tag. Very little Petit Syrah is grown in the region. Joseph's is approachable in its youth. It's not the weighty style you'd find from California, but good enough to impress any diehard fan of Rhone Valley wines. The Sherry is rich and complex, for cold winter days before a hearty meal. Joseph's icewines have won countless awards.

1811 Niagara Stone Road
N.O.T.L. ON L0S 1J0

T   905.468.1259
    1.866.468.1259 (toll free)
F   905.468.9242
W   www.josephsestatewines.com

ANNUAL PRODUCTION
32,000 cases

ACREAGE
20

WHEN TO VISIT
June to October
Daily 10–7

November to May
Daily 10–6

LCBO AVAILABILITY
None, at winery only, restaurants across Ontario, delivery in Ontario

KACABA VINEYARDS

On the south side of King Street across from the Vinehaven Bakery, you'll find the entrance to Kacaba Vineyards, marked by a large blue sign with white lettering. Drive past the sugar maple trees and you'll cross over a small silver bridge. Don't be alarmed by any sounds you hear during your crossing as it is rumoured to be designed to hold a tank! Drive up to the small mustard-coloured building and you'll quickly find the retail tasting room.

What was once a rolling horse farm now holds one of the region's first plantings of Syrah. In 1997, Mike Kacaba liberated this property that was slated for subdivision by the nearby town of Vineland. The wine-making duties are shared between consultant Jim Warren and Rob Warren (no family relation). Production is small and there's no plan to exceed 12,000 cases. Only a handful of staff manages the vineyard and winery. It's not uncommon to see Mike Kacaba and/or family on the weekends.

Kacaba makes one of the region's few Viogniers. Fresh, lean and delicious. The Pinot Noir here is well balanced and elegant. Drink alone or with fellow oenophiles!

3550 King Street
Vineland ON L0R 2C0

T 905.562.5625
F 905.562.1111
W www.kacaba.com

ANNUAL PRODUCTION
5,000 cases

ACREAGE
20

WHEN TO VISIT
May to October
Daily 10–6

November to April
Daily 11–5

LCBO AVAILABILITY
At winery only, delivery in Ontario

KITTLING RIDGE ESTATE WINES & SPIRITS

Kittling Ridge Estate Wines & Spirits is located off the QEW, near the Casablanca Exit 71, on the South Service Road. You'll notice the large scale of the beige building as you pull into the parking lot. Believe it or not, this unassuming building houses Ontario's third largest winery, and one of the only privately-owned distilleries in Canada. In 1971, the building was constructed by Swiss stillmaster, Otto Rieder. Built to withstand a blast from an exploding alcohol mishap, this facility specialized in fruit brandies, vodka and whiskies.

In 1992, Otto retired and John Hall stepped in as CEO. Soon after, in 1993, the facility got a commercial winery licence and changed its name from Rieder Distillery to Kittling Ridge. In the decade to follow, John Hall would grow both the wine and spirit portfolio substantially.

The winery now moves 60,000 cases from seven retail stores in the Grimsby and Toronto areas. The distillery side of the business has received serious international attention. The company exports are huge, selling more whisky in Texas than all the rest of Canada! They also sell to Asian, European and South American markets.

Winemaker/distiller John Hall continues to develop unique products with his team of 120 employees. In 2002, the company finished the expansion of a 50,000-square-foot cellar holding an almost inconceivable 22,000 barrels. The name "Kittling" derives from an expression for the circling movements of migratory birds that ride the thermal updrafts above the Niagara Escarpment.

SOMMELIER'S PICKS

John's wines are ready for consumption upon release, their price points hard to beat. Marechal Foch and the Riesling-Gewurztraminer are among my favourites. If you enjoy whisky, try the Forty Creek Barrel Select. This fantastic beverage was named after the community called "The Forty." Believing their settlement to be 40 miles from the mouth of Niagara Falls, early-1700s settlers built grist mills to process the fertile region's grain. Produced in small batches in a copper "pot" still, this rich spirit oozes vanilla, spice and a toasty oak aroma. Its handcrafted quality is a steal at half the cost of well-known Canadian Reserve whiskies.

297 South Service Road
Grimsby ON L3M 1Y6

T   905.945.9225
F   905.945.4330
W   www.kittlingridge.com

ANNUAL PRODUCTION
60,000 cases

ACREAGE
None, 100% of fruit is purchased
from local growers

WHEN TO VISIT
Monday to Saturday 10–6,
Sundays and Holidays 11–5

LCBO AVAILABILITY
Yes, some products available only
at the winery

KONZELMANN ESTATE WINERY

Driving on Lake Shore Road west of the Old Town of Niagara-on-the-Lake you'll find Konzelman Estate Winery. At the north end of the parking area you'll discover a stepped rock outcropping from which there is a great vantage point overlooking the property's vineyards, Lake Ontario and the Toronto skyline. This is one of the region's few waterfront settings. Herbert Konzelmann has worked in the wine trade since 1958, starting at the winery his great grandfather established in the late 1800s near Stuttgart, Germany. Recognizing new prospects in the Niagara wine industry, Herbert immigrated to Canada in 1984 to establish the winery on the current site. Herbert brought in winemaker Matthias Boss in 2000 to help out with expanding production. Trained at the Wiensburg Oenology School in Germany, Matthias has more than a decade of production experience in Europe. Visit during one of the winery's many weekend BBQs.

Herbert makes some serious Gewurztraminer. Pinot Blanc is great and should be enjoyed with your grandma's choucroute. Reserve Merlot is a consistent and reliable deal, year in, year out.

1096 Lakeshore Road R.R. 3
N.O.T.L. ON L0S 1J0

T 905.935.2866
F 905.935.2864
W www.konzelmannwines.com

ANNUAL PRODUCTION
35,000 cases

ACREAGE
83

WHEN TO VISIT
May to October
Daily 10–6, Sunday 12–6

November to April
Daily 11–5, Sunday 12–5

LCBO AVAILABILITY
Yes, some reserves at winery only, delivery in Canada, some U.S. states and Asia

LAILEY VINEYARD AND WINERY

Driving along the Niagara Parkway, across from the historic McFarland House, you'll see a small, discreet green sign with white lettering marked Lailey Vineyard and Winery. Drive down the short gravel lane and discover some of Niagara's best wines. The 20-acre property is owned by Donna and David Lailey. The land was acquired by David's father, William, in the early 1950s when hybrid grapes were grown along with other tender fruit.

After taking over the farm in 1970, Donna and David began removing the orchard and planting vinifera grape varieties. The harvested grapes and juice were sold to commercial and home winemakers. Truly a wine industry pioneer, Donna is one of the founding members of the VQA and was named "Grape Queen" in 1991, an honour awarded by the Ontario Grape Growers' Marketing Board for the best vineyard. Over the years, Lailey Vineyard established a good relationship with winemaker Derek Barnett of Southbrook Winery in Toronto. In 2001, a partnership was formed and Derek made the move to the newly-built facility.

Derek makes wines with distinct character and depth. His wines are anything but shy, and are best accompanied by food flavours that can match the wines' intensity. The soil of the vineyard is a sandy loam with clay and shale subsoil. The Lailey team has discovered that canopy management techniques specific to each grape variety work well on this vineyard site. Although this proves to be labour-intensive, they consider it valuable because they attribute the quality of their wine to the quality of fruit in the vineyard.

Derek processes all grape varietals in small batches and is able to experiment with wild yeast fermentation and Canadian oak aging. Production is small and will stay that way since expanding would mean sourcing fruit from other growers. An unwavering commitment to quality has earned the Lailey crew a passionate customer following. When visiting, don't be surprised to meet patrons who have driven great distances to pick up cases of these wines!

All of Derek's wines are well made; however, one of his favourite varietals to work with is Pinot Noir, and it shows. His Sauvignon Blanc is made in a fresh, crisp style, wonderful with summer-time shellfish. Buy as much as you can of his Cabernet Franc, as it's one of the region's finest examples of how weighty, powerful and complex this wine can become in a cool climate like Niagara.

15940 Niagara Parkway
N.O.T.L. ON L0S 1J0

T   905.468.0503
F   905.468.8012
W   www.laileyvineyard.com

ANNUAL PRODUCTION
6,000 cases

ACREAGE
20

WHEN TO VISIT
May to October
Daily 10–6, Sundays 11–5

November to April
Daily 11–5

LCBO AVAILABILITY
None in stores, some products available through the Vintages catalogue

LAKEVIEW CELLARS
ESTATE WINERY

Drive a few hundred feet south onto Cherry Avenue from King Street and you could very easily drive past a small wooden sign on your left marked Lakeview Cellars. Behind the beige one-and-a-half-storey home is a small gravel parking lot next to a large green, metal-clad building. The facility you see today has been renovated to accommodate a growing portfolio. The Bench property was purchased by Eddy and Lorraine Gurinskas in 1986. Eddy had been a longtime amateur winemaker when Lakeview Cellars Winery was founded in 1991, with 2,300 cases.

In 2000, Diamond Wines entered the scene as a partner and is now selling their wines in 10 provinces. Eddy was honoured with the Winemaker of the Year award in 2003 at the Ontario Wine Awards. Soon after this recognition, he passed the torch to Tom Green. With solid chemistry, viticulture and oenology training from University of Western Ontario and Brock University, Tom brings energy and knowledge to Lakeview Cellars. He also oversees production at the sister winery, Birchwood Estate.

Tom is well known for his Bordeaux-style reds and aromatic whites. His Riesling is always a good buy. Reserve Chardonnay is a bold, rich food wine, a frequent award-winner. If you're feeling hedonistic, try the Reserve Baco Noir. This monster red is sure to please any Baco fan. In the mood for Port anyone? The "Starboard" is high-quality Cabernet Sauvignon that has been treated like the great fortified wine from Portugal's Douro Valley. Its over-the-top powerful style would match well with stinky blue cheese.

4037 Cherry Avenue
Vineland ON L0R 2C0

T 905.562.5685
F 905.562.0673
W www.lakeviewcellars.on.ca

ANNUAL PRODUCTION
22,000 cases

ACREAGE
13

WHEN TO VISIT
May to October
Daily 10–5:30

November to April
Daily 10–5

LCBO AVAILABILITY
Chardonnay, Gewurztraminer and Baco make regular appearances. Reserve wines often available through the Vintages catalogue. Delivery in Ontario

LEGENDS ESTATE WINERY

Located a few hundred metres north of the QEW, past the North Service Road on Ontario Street in Beamsville (Exit 64) you'll see a large sign directing you to one of the region's few waterfront winery sites. In 1946, John Lizak purchased this 40-acre property and farmed tender fruit. Today, John's son Ted and grandson Paul farm this site as well as two other nearby properties. Find a parking spot in the large lot and head toward the rectangular metal-sided building that was once used to store equipment and fruit. Consultant winemaker Andre Lipinski is crafting some exceptional wine here. Trained as a mechanic in Poland, he turned to winemaking; now his reputation as a 1998 VinItaly award winner precedes him. A large portion of production is still fruit wine but will change as more of the 30 acres of young vineyards come on line. Expect to see more awards pile up for this young winery.

Andre's Gewurztraminer is a fantastic buy, a rich and wildly aromatic wine to enjoy with your favourite spicy Asian foods. The Pinot Noir has good weight and intensity. The Bordeaux-style reds are huge. Look for Malbec planted on the waterfront in 2003! The dry plum wine is a local favourite.

4888 Ontario Street North
Beamsville ON L0R 1B3

T   905.563.6500
F   905.563.1672
W www.legendsestates.com

ANNUAL PRODUCTION
18,000 cases

ACREAGE
200

WHEN TO VISIT
May to November
Daily 10–7

December to April
Weekends only 10–7

LCBO AVAILABILITY
At winery only, delivery in Ontario

MAGNOTTA ESTATE WINERY

Located on the east side of Ontario Street near the QEW in Beamsville, this is only one of seven Magnotta locations. Magnotta is no small company. They produce and sell wine, beer, spirits, grape juice and winemaking supplies and are publicly traded on the Toronto Stock Exchange. Gabe and Rosanna Magnotta built this company into one of the region's largest producers from the ground up. Since 1985, the couple has been importing juice for home winemakers. In the late 1980s, an opportunity to purchase Charal Winery in Blenheim, Ontario, led to a rapid expansion to more than a hundred products and the purchase in 1996 of 150 vineyard acres in Niagara and 350 in Chile.

Marco Zamuner and his team oversee a huge production, all of which is sold without the help of the LCBO. The Beamsville location is large and airy. Attentive and knowledgeable staff will help you make a great selection.

SOMMELIER'S PICKS

The Viognier is made in a light, lean style loaded with citrus aroma and flavour. At less than $10, you can't beat it. Drink with lots of peel-and-eat shrimp! Cabernet Franc limited edition is a good buy here as well. For grappa fans, this is your stop. The on-site "still" is used for making this grappa from used Cabernet Franc icewine skins. Sniff, sip and slurp with espresso after a rich meal with good friends.

4701 Ontario Street
Beamsville ON L0R 1B0

T 905.563.5313
   1.800.461.9463 (toll free)
F 905.563.8804
W www.magnotta.com

ANNUAL PRODUCTION
450,000 cases, company wide

ACREAGE
180

WHEN TO VISIT
Daily 9–6
Sunday 11–5

LCBO AVAILABILITY
No, winery and retail locations
only, delivery in Ontario

MALETA ESTATE WINERY

Driving west on Queenston Road you'll find Maleta Estate Winery on the north side, just past Townline Road. As you enter from either side of the steep circular drive, you can't miss the maroon-painted Quonset hut that houses the production facility. The tasting room is in the western side of the brick home, where you can also view works of art by local artist John Newby. The winery was opened in 1998 by retired car dealer Stan Maleta and his wife Marilyn. It's possible that this winery site was one of Niagara's first commercial vineyards, believed to have been developed in the mid-1800s by the long-gone Sunnieholme Winery, which was located just down the road. Stan attributes the quality of his wines to the work in the vineyard. Fruit is cut away throughout the growing season to a measure of two tons to the acre. This is approximately half the average of the region.

Inside the Quonset hut, Stan has craftily employed the small space and used both French and American oak to achieve complexity in his wines. In 2004, Daniel Pambianchi, of Cadenza wines, bought the winery. Don't worry—Stan is still the winemaker.

SOMMELIER'S PICKS

Riesling is made here in a rich and lavish style. Stan's favourite wines to make are big bold Bordeaux-style reds, and it shows. Meritage is King here; enjoy it with grilled T-bones. Look for Syrah to be released in 2005.

450 Queenston Road
N.O.T.L. ON L0S 1J0

T   905.685.8486
F   905.685.7998
W   www.maletawinery.com

ANNUAL PRODUCTION
3,000 cases

ACREAGE
17

WHEN TO VISIT
May to October
Daily 10:30–5:30, except Tuesday and Wednesday

November to April
Weekends only 11–5

LCBO AVAILABILITY
At winery only, delivery in Ontario

MALIVOIRE WINE COMPANY

Across the road from Thomas & Vaughan Vintners, on the south side of King Street east of Beamsville, drive up a small gravel road past a well-landscaped entrance and you'll find what looks like a three-storey-Quonset hut built up a hillside.

Malivoire Wine Company is owned by Martin Malivoire and partner Moira Saganski. In 1995, the couple purchased a vineyard east of Beamsville, pursuing a lifelong dream to build a weekend wine-country retreat from successful and busy lives in Toronto. Three years later, a second vineyard was purchased and new grape varietals were planted.

The winery was designed to take advantage of the ravine. Built down a hillside, seven different levels allow for winemaking without the use of pumps. This is a gentle process that has been used in Europe for centuries but is new to Niagara.

Production is small, with grapes sourced primarily from Malivoire's own vineyards in which biodynamic grape-growing techniques are used. Instead of insecticides and herbicides, natural deterrents are used for threats to the vines, and all vineyard work is completed meticulously by hand. Wood posts are even used instead of metal, to avoid negatively affecting the microclimate of the vines!

Winegrower Ann Sperling was raised on an Okanagan B.C. vineyard where her family has grown grapes for more than a century. Ann has been making wine since the early 1990s and has brought a wealth of knowledge to Malivoire. Her determination in the vineyard certainly shows in the high-quality wines she produces. All of this hard work and experience earned her Winemaker of the Year at the Ontario Wine Awards in 2004.

The Moira Vineyard Chardonnay is marvelous and elegant. Full, rich and well balanced with citrus fruits and acidity, this is one of Niagara's highest-quality Chardonnays. You can't visit Niagara without sampling Old Vines Foch, a massive and weighty wine for Niagara. I've found that tasters either love or hate this wine, a great pairing for rich meats and game. The Riesling icewine, packaged conveniently in 200-millilitre bottles, leaves the palate refreshed.

4260 King Street
Beamsville ON L0R 1B0

T 905.563.9253
   1.866.644.2244 (toll free)
F 905.563.9512
W www.malivoirewineco.com

ANNUAL PRODUCTION
10,000 cases

ACREAGE
60

WHEN TO VISIT
Monday to Friday 10–5
Weekends 11–5

January and February
by appointment

LCBO AVAILABILITY
At winery only, delivery in Ontario.
Some products available through
the Vintages catalogue

MARYNISSEN ESTATES WINERY

Off the beaten path, driving down Concession 1, you'll stumble across Marynissen Estates Winery between Line 3 and Larkin Road. The lane from the road will drop you in front of a short, wide outbuilding sided with vertical pine. Pass through the white doorway to taste from the oldest Cabernet Sauvignon vines in Canada.

In 1952, John and Nanny Marynissen emigrated from Holland to grow grapes in Niagara. Thinking forward, John planted a small block of Cabernet Sauvignon vines in 1978, now known as Lot 66. At the age of 65, John developed a plan to build the winery. Now in his 80s, John has passed the torch to daughter Sandra and son-in-law Glen.

John has little to worry about with the new team, although he is known to "supervise" on occasion. Grapes are sourced only from their 70 acres of sandy loam soil located in one of the hottest areas of the Niagara-on-the-Lake macroclimate. Glen attributes the success of his big reds to this fact, combined with a "get it right the first time" attitude in production.

Dedication to quality is paramount here, and it shows in the flavour and texture of the wines. Sandra and Glen simply refuse to rush the process. Marynissen has a small but extremely loyal clientele. If you're ever in Ottawa and invited to dinner with the Governor-General, don't be surprised to find Marynissen wines served with your meal.

SOMMELIER'S PICKS

You can't beat the value of Marynissen's Cabernet Merlot blend—year in, year out a steal under $15. All the reserve reds are good value if you consider the small amount of production. Ask general manager Ann McIntyre about their Syrah and Petit Syrah. These wines are neither advertised nor available for tasting. If you're lucky, you may be led through the winery to a small dark room to buy a couple of bottles. Micro-amounts of these wines are made from young but promising vineyards. These wines are half the cost of those by some of the region's other producers of red Rhone-styled varietals.

R.R. 6, 1208 Concession 1
N.O.T.L. ON L0S 1J0

T 905.468.7270
F 905.468.5784
W www.marynissen.com

ANNUAL PRODUCTION
10,000 cases

ACREAGE
70

WHEN TO VISIT
May to October
Daily 10–6

November to April
Daily 10–5

LCBO AVAILABILITY
None, delivery in Ontario

MOUNTAIN ROAD WINE COMPANY

As you arrive in the small town of Beamsville, drive south up Mountain Street toward the top of the Escarpment. A kilometre up the road, you'll find a large oak tree with a shaded sign directing you past an old barn to a large brick home and outbuildings. Mountain Road Wine Company sits on one of the Kocsis family's three vineyards.

Steve Kocsis is a long-time, high-quality grape grower. Over the last 20 years, he has sold grapes to Chateau Des Charmes, Cave Spring, Thirty Bench and Inniskillin, to name a few. Grapes sourced from his vineyards have taken top awards at competition and were represented in the first Ontario Chardonnay released in the LCBO Vintages catalogue.

In the late 1990s, Steve became increasingly frustrated with relationships between grape growers and wineries. This dilemma prompted him to start producing his own wines. However, his troubles didn't stop there. Due to urban development in Beamsville, the Kocsis' 45-acre farm had been designated subdividable land by the Town of Lincoln. After several years of hearings and committee meetings, he was finally permitted the now 500-square-foot retail boutique in the walk-out cellar of the large family home. The winery opened to the public in the fall of 2003.

This is truly a family enterprise. Son Richard is involved with vineyard management, and daughter Joanna is in charge of marketing and promotion. Steve has also enlisted the help of hard-working winemaker Jon Witowski, a Niagara College Graduate. The wines are made from premium grapes grown on the family's own Hillside Drive and Fly Road vineyards. A large inventory of wine is available for such a seemingly small winery. One thing is for certain; expect big things from this little winery.

SOMMELIER'S PICKS

There's fantastic value in Chardonnay at this winery. Sourced from old vines, the result is well-balanced wine. Harmonious fruit, acidity and buttery oak make these wines a steal under $20. The 2000 Chardonnay Reserve placed second at the 2004 Cuvee awards. For those of you who are Baco fans, pick up a case here for the wine rack!

4016 Mountain Street
Beamsville ON L0R 1B7

T 905.563.0745
F 905.563.0650
W www.mountainroadwine.com

ANNUAL PRODUCTION
2,000 cases

ACREAGE
45

WHEN TO VISIT
Monday to Saturday 10–6
Sunday 11–5

LCBO AVAILABILITY
At winery only

NIAGARA COLLEGE
TEACHING WINERY

I have to admit it, I've found some great wines in the most unexpected place: school. Across from the White Oaks Resort and Spa, on the corner of Glendale Avenue and Taylor Road, you'll find the Glendale Campus of Niagara College. After entering the complex, follow the signs to the wine store. Currently this is Canada's only teaching winery. The wines are actually made by 25 full-time, hard-working students in the large, brown, hip-roofed barn on the eastern edge of the campus. Students are coached by winemaking professor Jim Warren, and care for all the winery procedures, from pruning vines and pressing grapes to operating the retail store. Production is small and will grow at the rate of the program. While you're there, book yourself in for a meal next door, at the Niagara Culinary Institute Dining Room. With fantastic flavours at discounted prices, your meal is prepared by Niagara's rising culinary stars. On your way out, you may want to hit the retail horticulture store for some garden deals.

SOMMELIER'S PICKS

The barrel-aged Chardonnay is rich and oaky, a big white that works well with grilled fish with hearty sauces. The Sauvignon Blanc is fun and fresh. The Meritage is an ogre, needing several years in the cellar to soften those tannins.

135 Taylor Road
N.O.T.L. ON L0S 1J0

T 905.641.2252 ext 4070
F 905.988.4317
W www.nctwinery.com

ANNUAL PRODUCTION
2,500 cases

ACREAGE
38

WHEN TO VISIT
Monday to Saturday 10–5
Sunday 11–5

LCBO AVAILABILITY
At winery only, delivery in Ontario

PALATINE HILLS ESTATE WINERY

Driving along the scenic Lakeshore Road, be sure to make the time to stop at Palatine Hills Estate Winery. On the south side of the road you'll see a large yellow sign directing you toward a metal-dressed building. The facility is run by long-time grape growers John and Barbara Neufeld. This farm is large, running from Lakeshore south, backing onto the East/West Line. Grapes and juice had previously been sold to wineries nearby and in Pennsylvania and New York States, until an excess of icewine juice in 1998 allowed John to graduate from amateur winemaker with the help of winemaking consultant David Hojnoski. Since that time, awards have piled up, production has skyrocketed and the facility has had an extensive expansion.

David's food and price-friendly wines show loads of promise. To all you amateur winemakers out there, high-quality grape juice, use of on-site facilities and lab work are available to you.

The Proprietors Reserve Chardonnay is rich and sleek—excellent value. Reserve reds are big and bold, and the reserve Merlot is particularly outstanding. Gewurztraminer icewine is an opulent steal! Loaded with tropical fruit and superb balance, this is sure to impress any icewine lover.

911 Lakeshore Road
N.O.T.L. ON L0S 1J0

T 905.646.9617
F 905.646.5832
W www.palatinehillsestate
   winery.com

ANNUAL PRODUCTION
8,000 cases

ACREAGE
180

WHEN TO VISIT
May to October
Daily 10–6

November to April
Daily 10–5

LCBO AVAILABILITY
At winery only, delivery in Ontario

PELLER ESTATES WINERY

Driving along the East/West Line close to the Niagara Parkway, it's difficult to miss Peller Estates Winery. Situated amongst 25 acres of vineyard, this is one of the region's most romantic settings. Andrew and Lena Peller immigrated to Canada from Hungary in 1927. Soon after arriving, Andrew found employment at a brewery in Kitchener. Several years later, Peller's Brewery was established in Hamilton. In 1961, after many successful ventures outside the beer industry, Andrew moved to Port Moody, B.C., where Andres Wines was founded. By the late 1960s, son Joe had been pulled away from his medical practice to help guide this rapidly expanding business.

Today, grandson John is CEO of this publicly-traded company that is one Canada's largest producers of wine. The Peller Estates Winery opened in the spring of 2001 and houses one of Niagara-on-the-Lake's most exclusive restaurants. Private tasting rooms, old town shuttle service and comprehensive wine seminars set this winery apart from other large-scale facilities. Robert Summers has been making wine with the company since 1997. His wines are bold, fruit-forward and "new world" in style. The public tour through the winery's cellars offers some great information about the art of cooperage, or barrel making.

SOMMELIER'S PICKS

The Riesling here is a fresh, clean, good-value wine. The Gamay makes a great, inexpensive summer red. The Signature Series reds are massive, brooding wines with an equally intimidating price. Be prepared to lay them down in your cellar for some time. My favourite is the Cabernet Franc. Peller makes one of the region's few Cabernet Franc icewines, expensive even for icewine, but you'll be rewarded with lingering aromas of candied strawberry.

290 John Street East
N.O.T.L. ON L0S 1J0

T   905.468.4678
     1.888.673.5537 (toll free)
F   905.468.1920
W www.peller.com

ANNUAL PRODUCTION
40,000 cases

ACREAGE
25

WHEN TO VISIT
Daily 10–6

LCBO AVAILABILITY
Yes, 100 retail stores across Ontario, widely available across Canada

PENINSULA RIDGE ESTATES WINERY

Driving east from the town of Grimsby along King Street, you'll find one of the area's most romantic settings. Perched on the crest of a hill is a large red brick Victorian manor. Built in 1885, the Queen Anne revival building has become the signature image of Peninsula Ridge Winery and Restaurant.

Proprietor Norman Beal wanted to escape the busy and lucrative international oil trade. His schedule kept him away from his family and Connecticut home more than 40 weeks of the year! However, all this travelling did allow for exploration of some of the world's greatest wine regions. Raised in nearby Hamilton, Norman was visiting with family in 1998 when he first drove by the future winery property. It is rumoured that Norman simply knocked on the door, introduced himself, asked to view the property and made an offer "hard to refuse" on the 80-acre mixed fruit farm, house and falling-down outbuildings. Remarkably, 14 months and 6 million dollars later, the winery and restaurant opened in August of 2000.

The winery is surrounded by 45 acres of vineyard, but the facility sources the majority of its grapes from 11 different farms throughout Niagara. Peninsula Ridge has guaranteed farmers the sale of their grapes under 20-year contracts in return for permission to manage the vineyards to the winery's specifications. This process allows the winery to recognize vineyard sites that produce superior fruit and, ultimately, the best expression of Niagara grape varieties.

Peninsula Ridge also boasts a comprehensive barrel program. With exclusively sourced French oak from five different forests and coopers, the same small-batch quality that happens in the vineyard takes place in the cellar.

The whole facility produces a maximum 35,000 cases, so quality production will always be the focus. Winemaker Jean-Pierre Colas directs all this hands-on work. The restaurant is located in the signature brick home. Substantially renovated, this first-rate dining room maintains its original floor plan and boasts spectacular views of Lake Ontario and the Toronto skyline.

You must get your hands on some of Jean-Pierre's Sauvignon Blanc. Released in early spring, this is a fresh, clean S.B. with loads of citrus fruits. It always sells out quickly, so load up for the summer season. The reds are big and age-worthy. Reserve Cabernet Franc and Syrah are some of my favourites. The Ratafia, a different and delicious traditional Burgundian beverage, blends unfermented Chardonnay juice with locally distilled plum spirits.

5600 King Street West
Beamsville ON L0R 1B0

T 905.563.0900
F 905.563.0995
W www.peninsularidge.com

ANNUAL PRODUCTION
17,000 cases

ACREAGE
80

WHEN TO VISIT
May to October
Daily 10–6

November to April
11–5:30 on weekdays

LCBO AVAILABILITY
Yes, Chardonnay and Cabernet.
Reserve wines at facility only,
delivery in Ontario. Monthly "wine
club" service

PILLITTERI ESTATES WINERY

Driving along Niagara Stone Road (Highway 55), it's easy to spot the distinctive red buildings of Pillitteri Estates Winery, across from Mori Gardens, on the west side of the street. It's hard to imagine that this operation at one time sold only a few thousand cases of wine and local seasonal fruit. Pilliterri is now one of the region's largest estate producers of icewine, distributing across Canada and overseas.

Wines have been made here by Sue-Ann Staff since 1997. Sue-Ann has extensive viticulture and oenology training, both here in Ontario and Australia. Her family has been growing grapes in Niagara for generations and, in 2002, she was named Ontario's Winemaker of the Year.

This is still a family-run business. Gary and Lena Pillitteri opened the winery in 1993 after years of making amateur award-winning wines. Son Charlie, daughter Connie and son-in-law Jamie are involved in sales, operations and vineyard management. A large expansion of the facilities was completed in 2003 to accommodate growing production.

SOMMELIER'S PICKS

Sue-Ann's Reserve Cabernet Franc and Merlot are consistently outstanding. These are serious wines with loads of intensity, requiring medium-rare rib-eye steaks off the BBQ. The Pinot Grigio is a fresh, fun choice on hot summer patio days.

1686 Niagara Stone Road
N.O.T.L. ON L0R 1J0

T 905.468.3147
F 905.468.0389
W www.pillitteri.com

ANNUAL PRODUCTION
40,000 cases

ACREAGE
53

WHEN TO VISIT
May to October
Daily 10–8

November to April
Daily 10–6

LCBO AVAILABILITY
Yes, reserves and limited products at winery only, delivery in Ontario, many Canadian provinces, some U.S. states, Asia and Europe

PUDDICOMBE ESTATE WINES

The first winery on Niagara's wine route west of Grimsby has been in the Puddicombe family since 1797! Situated at the base of the Niagara Escarpment, this family-run operation has been growing grapes since 1940. The property is still largely committed to cherries, apples and raspberries for "pick your own" summertime harvesting. However, the eldest daughter, Lindsay Puddicombe, makes wine from grapes grown exclusively on their estate.

At 25, Lindsay is one of the region's youngest winemakers, but she is certainly making wines with promise. Her hard work has combined with training under winemakers Jim Warren and Sue-Ann Staff, and studies in agriculture at the University of Guelph and Niagara College, to bring Lindsay awards for both her fruit and table wines. Situated in what was the original site for Stoney Ridge wines, the winery produces 2,000 cases and is growing. This small winery also has a tea room café and general store offering local preserves, honey and other goodies. The warmth and hospitality of this centuries-old farm is certain to make you feel at home.

Lindsay's Sauvignon Blanc is bright and fresh, with loads of grassy and herbaceous notes. This wine would be well matched to steamed asparagus or light summer salads. Buy up as much as you can of her Viognier. Made in a light style, this is a fantastic summer sipper with tropical fruit notes. The raspberry fruit wine begs for rich, warm chocolate desserts.

1468 Highway 8
Winona ON L8E 5K9

T   905.643.1015
F   905.643.0938
W   www.puddicombefarms.com

ANNUAL PRODUCTION
2,000 cases

ACREAGE
300

WHEN TO VISIT
July to October
Daily 9–5

November to June
Wednesday to Sunday 9–5

LCBO AVAILABILITY
At winery only

REIF ESTATES WINERY

Driving along the Niagara Parkway, you'll find Reif Estates Winery situated next to the picturesque Grand Victorian B&B. Ewald Reif immigrated to Canada in 1977 from Neustadt Germany, where the Reif family has been making wine in the Pfalz since 1683.

Ewald's nephew Klaus now manages the operation at this facility, open to the public since 1983. A well-trained viticulturalist, Klaus oversees production in partnership with Roberto DiDomenico, who was brought on board in 1990. The property is large and well-situated close to the moderating influences of the Niagara River. Vineyard management is paramount here. Red varieties are especially crop-thinned to produce low-yielding, high-quality fruit. This vineyard is home to some of the region's few Zinfandel plantings.

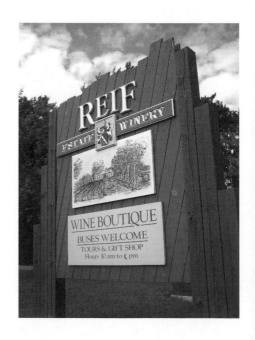

The general list Cabernet Merlot is one of the region's wines that offers value and consistency year after year at a great price point. The Rieslings are Germanic in style, with some modern edge. The "First Growth" line of reds has drawn some big attention. Older vines cropped at 2.5 tons an acre make these flagship wines serious, intricate and award-winning.

15608 Niagara Parkway
N.O.T.L. ON L0S 1J0

T 905.468.7738
F 905.468.5878
W www.reifwinery.com

ANNUAL PRODUCTION
40,000 cases

ACREAGE
135

WHEN TO VISIT
April to October
Daily 10–6

November to March
Daily 10–5

LCBO AVAILABILITY
Yes, delivery in Ontario

RIDGEPOINT WINES

Driving south up Cherry Avenue toward the top of the Escarpment, you'll find the entrance to Ridgepoint Wines on the west side of the road. The production facility, cellars and tasting boutique are located in two separate buildings a few hundred metres off the road, in the centre of the property's vineyard. Mauro and Anna Scarsellone purchased the property and started planting in 1995, keeping their operation small. All-new vineyard plantings and construction were completed by the end of 2004. This hard-working couple and their young children commute from their Mississauga home daily to oversee the operation. Winemaking consultant and oenologist Arthur Harder has helped out with the first few vintages. Arthur is a former winemaker at Hillebrand Estates Winery. Production will continue to be small and isn't likely to exceed 5,000 cases, as premium wines are the focus here. The winery's first claim to fame is having one of the region's first successful plantings of the Nebbiolo grape variety.

The well-textured, aromatic Riesling is made in both dry and off-dry style. If you're familiar with the "King of wines, the wine of Kings" from the Barolo region near Piedmonte in Northern Italy, the Nebbiolo is for you. Vegetarians beware! This monster wine begs for rich meat dishes, a "must have" with Nonna's braised lamb shanks.

3900 Cherry Avenue
Vineland ON L0R 2C0

T   905.562.8853
F   905.562.8854
W   www.ridgepointwines.com

ANNUAL PRODUCTION
2,000

ACREAGE
20

WHEN TO VISIT
May to October
Daily 10–6

November to April
weekends 10–6 or call ahead

LCBO AVAILABILITY
At winery only, delivery in Ontario

RIVERVIEW CELLARS

As you drive north along the Niagara Parkway from Niagara Falls, the first winery you'll discover after passing the village of Queenston is Riverview Cellars. This small winery is located on the west side of the road in a mushroom-coloured metal-clad building with white trim. Long-time growers Sam and Lena Pillitteri sold grapes for years to their relatives on Highway 55 at Pillitteri Estates Winery before opening this facility in 1998.

In the summer of 2004, Fred DiProfio took over as winemaker from Sam. Fred has worked with Sue-Ann Staff since 1999 and is soon to graduate from Brock University's viticulture program. Riverview will continue to run as a family operation; son Michael manages the facility.

A small tasting room also offers Canadian and Niagara specialty syrups, honeys, preserves and baked goods. Shop till you drop!

Vidal icewine is very good here. Icewine sourced from this vineyard has won huge international awards. The Reserve Cabernet Franc is loaded with berry fruit and well-structured tannins. Micro production, so buy while supplies last.

15376 Niagara Parkway
N.O.T.L. ON L0S 1J0

T 905.262.0636
F 905.262.0462
W www.riverviewcellars.com

ANNUAL PRODUCTION
5,000 cases

ACREAGE
20

WHEN TO VISIT
April to November
Daily 10–6

December to March
Daily 10–5

LCBO AVAILABILITY
At winery only, delivery in Ontario, most U.S. states and some international destinations

ROCKWAY GLEN ESTATE WINERY

Driving along Fourth Avenue or King Street, turn south up Ninth Street and follow signs to Rockway Glen Estate Winery and Golf Course. Located in a remote part of western St. Catharines, this is the region's only combined winery and golf course. Wines are made just across the street by Jeff Innes. The on-site vineyards were planted in 2002, so most of the fruit is sourced from other vineyards in the region. Production is expected to grow to 20,000 cases. The facility also houses the only wine museum in Canada. Seventeenth-century barrels, bottles, presses and other artifacts line the underground display area. The golf course offers excellent wine, dinner and golf packages throughout the season. Swing, sip and savour.

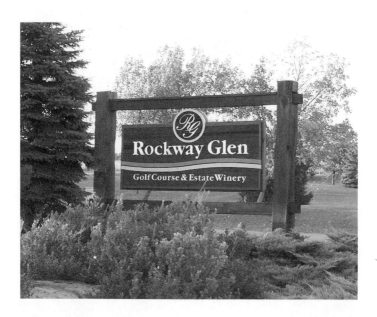

Floral and fruity, the Vidal is a fun crowd-pleaser, a great buy under $10. The Baco Noir is weighty and intense with earthy, leathery, licorice-root aromas. The Cabernet-Merlot blend is a good buy under $15. Special reserve reds are big, complex and undervalued.

3290 9th Street Louth R.R. 1
St. Catharines ON L2R 6P7

T 905.641.1030
   1.877.762.5929 (toll free)
F 905.641.2031
W www.rockwayglen.com

ANNUAL PRODUCTION
7,000 cases

ACREAGE
35

WHEN TO VISIT
May to October
Monday to Saturday 11–7
Sun 12–5

November to April
Daily 10–4

LCBO AVAILABILITY
At winery only, delivery in Ontario

ROYAL DEMARIA WINES

Driving along Cherry Avenue between Greenlane Road and John Street, look for Royal DeMaria on the east side of the road. Follow the long, narrow driveway, lined with old-fashioned streetlights, along a small wooded area to a blue outbuilding. The property was acquired in the early 1990s by Joseph DeMaria, who still works at his successful hair salon in Toronto. Joseph's first vintage was in 1998.

The whole operation is devoted to the production of our winter wonder, icewine. It's rumoured that a few steps in the fermentation and aging process are omitted to create a "secret recipe" that separate Joseph's wines from the competition. All of the 12 icewines are made from fruit grown on the property, with the exception of Pinot Gris and Muscat Ottonel. The volume of domestic and international awards is staggering and warrants the company's motto, Canada's Icewine Specialists. You may want to brace yourself before getting a look at the reserve pricelist. With price tags from $60 to $5,000, these are truly Canada's most expensive wines. The customer database includes Queen Elizabeth, who has ordered for delivery. The winery has come a long way from its humble beginnings of crafting the first vintage on a dirt floor in the building that now consists of the medal showroom, tasting bar and production area, where renovations are ongoing.

SOMMELIER'S PICKS

The Vidal is one of the best sellers, not surprising as it has the smallest price tag. The Gewurztraminer and Muscat Ottonel are among my favourites, rich and complex, with lively acidity and extreme length on the palate, everything an icewine should be.

Joseph, say hello to Her Majesty for us!

4551 Cherry Avenue
Beamsville ON L0R 1B1

T 905.562.6767
   1.888.793.8883 (toll free)
F 905.562.6775
W www.royaldemaria.com

ANNUAL PRODUCTION
1,200 cases

ACREAGE
25

WHEN TO VISIT
April to October
Daily 11–6, Sunday 11–5

November to March
by appointment only

LCBO AVAILABILITY
At winery only, delivery in Ontario, some U.S. states and some countries

STONECHURCH VINEYARDS

Stonechurch is located a few hundred metres off Lakeshore Road, near the Welland Canal. Turn down Irvine Road and you'll find it on the west side of the street. This property is actually one of the largest family-run vineyards in the Niagara region. It's been farmed for more than 40 years by the Hunse family, with vinifera varieties planted in 1972 by Lambert and Grace Hunse. Son Rick and daughter-in-law Fran founded the winery in 1990. It's named after a church built by Empire Loyalists on Irvine Road in the 1850s. The soil varies in consistency from heavy clay to gravel and silt. This soil variation combined with biodynamic practices has contributed to the success and quality of these wines.

From the exterior, the retail shop is deceivingly small, yet the winery boasts a hospitality room that can hold 100 guests. There's a self-guided vineyard tour available, great to combine with one of the winery's many weekend summertime BBQs.

The Morio Muscat is a great summer sipper. Loads of floral and fruity notes have made this one of Stonechurch's benchmark wines. There's some good value in the reserve reds, loads of complexity at a great price. The winery is also known for last-minute selloff deals.

1242 Irvine Road
N.O.T.L. ON L0S 1J0

T 905.935.3535
   866.935.3500 (toll free)
F 905.646.8892
W www.stonechurch.com

ANNUAL PRODUCTION
30,000 cases

ACREAGE
200

WHEN TO VISIT
May to October
Monday to Saturday 10–7
Sunday 11–5

November to April
Daily 11–5

LCBO AVAILABILITY
At winery only, delivery in Ontario

STONEY RIDGE ESTATE WINERY

Driving east along King Street passing through the tiny town of Vineland, you'll quickly find yourself approaching Stoney Ridge Estate Winery on the north side of the road. The property is somewhat un-assuming as you pull into the gravel parking lot and walk past a large metal-clad building toward a renovated home used as retail and administration offices. Stoney Ridge stems from one of the region's winemaking pioneers. In 1985, local wine legend Jim Warren started making and selling wine from a property on Ridge Road in Stoney Creek. Sourcing fruit from international and local high-quality producers, Jim built a loyal clientele, pushing his production to 4,000 cases sold out of a garage! In 1989, Jim formed a partnership with Murray Puddicombe. With more space and winemaking equipment, production grew to 26,000 cases by 1997. After the winery moved to its current location, Jim decided to retire in 2000, passing the torch to Liubomir Popovici. From 1995 to 1999, Liubomir was the winemaker at Romania's largest wine and spirit producer. He has brought a wealth of knowledge and enthusiasm to Stoney Ridge. His wines are elegant and well-structured, with a boutique feel, even though production bobs around 40,000 cases.

In the late 1990s, Stoney Ridge expanded the production facility and increased estate vineyard holdings significantly, allowing for complete control over vineyard fruit quality. Liubomir combines fruit sourced from the estate and nearby vineyards with new-world technology and old-world know-how to create a portfolio of wines that gets attention and acclaim from critics and peers alike.

SOMMELIER'S PICKS

You must try Liubomir's Pinot Grigio, named for its Italian style. Pick up a case of this ultimate patio sipper and consume daily! There's also the more serious unwooded Charlotte's Chardonnay. Legend has it that Jim Warren first crafted this wine for his wife, who didn't care for Chardonnay with the usual woody flavours. The Cabernet Franc is also great value here in the "Bench" series everyday drinking wines and the reserve category, especially from the Wismer & Kew vineyards. Buy and hold.

3201 King Street
Vineland ON L0R 2C0

T 905.562.1324
F 905.562.7777
W www.stoneyridge.com

ANNUAL PRODUCTION
40,000 cases

ACREAGE
240

WHEN TO VISIT
July to August
Daily 10–6

September to June
Daily 10–5

LCBO AVAILABILITY
Yes, some reserve wines at winery only

STREWN ESTATE WINERY

At the corner of Four Mile Creek Road and Lakeshore, you'll find Strewn Winery, housed in the abandoned Niagara Canning Company. This concrete-block facility was built in the 1930s. After canned goods fell out of favour, the building was used as a warehouse for decades.

Winemaker Joe Will and partners opened the doors after extensive restorations in 1997. The winery is now home to a recreational cooking school offering classes for couples as well as social and corporate groups. Classes are led by long-time foodie Jane Langdon. Also located within the winery is Terrior La Cachette restaurant, guided by chef Alain Levesque and maitre d' Tricia Keyes.

After years in the corporate world, Joe Will left to study his craft in Adelaide, Australia. A short stint working vineyards in British Columbia followed, and by the early 1990s Joe was back in Ontario making wine at nearby Pillitteri. Joe's first vintage under the Strewn label was actually 1994, even though the facility was not open to the public until 1997. Fruit is sourced from the estate and contracted vineyards within 10 kilometres of the winery. The production area is huge, with the capacity to more than double the current wine amount. The company's cellars are lined with barrels funded by individuals who have invested in them in return for annual wine purchases in the retail store. The Barrel Club is an ingenious way for a small wine company to finance pricey wood aging vessels.

What you'll also appreciate about Strewn is the depth of wine product available to purchase. Young wineries, due to financial or production restraints, usually offer wines only from the previous year's vintage. Joe ages many wines in bottle at the winery, and it isn't uncommon to be able to purchase wine with two to seven years of bottle age. It's no wonder this is such a popular stop along the wine route. Strewn's winery, restaurant and cooking school truly have something to offer any food and wine lover.

Joe is best known for his big Cabernet and blended reds that are carefully handled and Bordeaux-inspired, with complex subtleties. His Riesling has fantastic elegance and balance, and is wonderfully ageworthy. There's fantastic value in Joe's late-harvested wines. Become a member of the Barrel Club and enjoy these wines for years to come!

1339 Lakeshore Road
N.O.T.L. ON L0S 1J0

T 905.468.1229
F 905.468.8305
W www.strewnwinery.com

ANNUAL PRODUCTION
17,000 cases

ACREAGE
26

WHEN TO VISIT
Daily 10–6

LCBO AVAILABILITY
Cabernet-Merlot, Riesling Gewurztraminer at select stores, some Vintage catalogue selections, reserve wines at winery only, delivery in Ontario

SUNNYBROOK FARM ESTATE WINERY

For those of you who have turned your noses up at your uncle's home-made elderberry wine, prepare to be converted. Just a few hundred metres east of Strewn winery on Lakeshore Road, you'll see a small green and gold sign marked "Sunnybrook Farm Estate Wines" leading you to a small gravel parking area. Gerald and Vivien Goertz and their daughter Rebecca operate the region's only fruit winery. Gerald has worked in orchards and made fruit wine since he was a teenager. Years ago, a hail storm damaged tens of thousands of dollars worth of fruit. Gerald ended up turning the tons of apples and peaches into wine. The wine is made in an outbuilding a few hundred feet from the tiny tasting boutique. All of Gerald's wines are Quality Certified (QC). This designation is the equivalent of the VQA for grape wines. Production and growing methods are closely monitored for quality, and all products are reviewed by a tasting panel. All of the fruit comes from the winery site, with the exception of berries. Studies from the University of Guelph claim that fruit wines contain more vitamins and minerals than grape wines.

The Ironwood Hard Cider blows the doors off imported products. The apricot wine is a best-seller, and the black currant and black raspberry have bold, intense, long-lasting flavours. Pair with your favourite chocolate pâté.

1425 Lakeshore Road R.R. 3
N.O.T.L. ON L0S 1J0

T 905.468.1122
F 905.468.1068
W www.sunnybrookfarm
   winery.com

ANNUAL PRODUCTION
4,500 cases

ACREAGE
11

WHEN TO VISIT
March to November
Daily 10–5

January to February
Thursday to Monday 10–5

LCBO AVAILABILITY
At winery only, delivery in Ontario

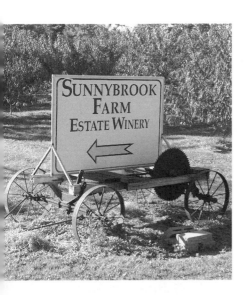

THIRTEENTH STREET WINERY

Of all the wineries in Niagara, you won't find one shrouded with more mystique and celebrity than Thirteenth Street Winery. Fans of this winery will describe their experience with a dazzling Thirteenth Street Pinot Noir like a religious experience. As the name indicates, the winery is located on Thirteenth Street just off of Fourth Avenue, west of St. Catharines. Don't blink or you may miss the small shingle on the east side of the road.

In 1998, partners Ken Douglas, Irv Willms, Gunther Funk and Herb Jacobson formed this kibbutz-style operation where winemaking facilities, vineyards and knowledge are shared to make wines under the G.H. Funk, Sandstone and 13th Street labels. Fruit is sourced from the partners' vineyards on the winery site and Niagara-on-the-Lake. Specific grape varieties have been selected for each site according to their different soil structures and mesoclimates. For those of you who plan to stock your cellars with these hard-to-get wines, don't get your hopes too high. It's likely that production will continue to float around 1,500 cases.

SOMMELIER'S PICKS

These wines are adored by enthusiasts and wine industry peers alike. The Sparkling wine is a steal at $25. Pinot Noir and Gamay are fantastic. Both are complex, well-balanced and fruit-forward. Buy. Hold. Sell to fanatics on eBay for a small fortune.

3983 13th Street
Jordan Station ON L0R 1S0

T 905.562.9463
F 905.562.8766
W www.13thstreetwines.com

ANNUAL PRODUCTION
1,500 cases

ACREAGE
28

WHEN TO VISIT
Most Saturdays 11–5, or by chance. Be sure to call or email ahead.

LCBO AVAILABILITY
At winery only, delivery in Ontario

THIRTY BENCH
VINEYARD & WINERY

Driving south up Mountainview Road off King Street, you will quickly come to the entrance of Thirty Bench on your left-hand side. A long, dusty driveway leads you to a weather-beaten wood-sided building surrounded by well-established vineyards. Don't be surprised to be greeted by a friendly dog or two.

In 1980, the original property was purchased and planted with Riesling by owners/winemakers Tom Muckle, Yorgos Papageorgiou and Franz Zeritsch. The first vintage wasn't produced until the early '90s. Riesling is still the dominant grape here, although, with a significant increase in acreage holdings in 2000, more reds are expected to move into the portfolio. The facility name derives from the nearby Thirty Mile Creek and ideal Bench location. The vineyard is micro-managed by Marek Maniecki and his crew, who favour crop-thinning to increase flavour and quality of grapes by harvest time. At the spacious tasting bar, you'll notice the variations of varietal wine styles. The Rieslings are made in dry, off-dry, sweet, low-alcohol, barrel-aged and icewine to name a few. Something for everyone!

The Benchmark reds and Reserve Chardonnays are serious, complex, age-worthy and expensive. Riesling is always great here and represents good value. My favourite is the semi-dry. Enjoy it with curry-flavoured soups. The Canadian Oaked Cabernet Franc is excellent.

4281 Mountainview Road
Beamsville ON L0R 1B0

T   905.563.1698
F   905.563.3921
W   www.thirtybench.com

ANNUAL PRODUCTION
8,500 cases

ACREAGE
68

WHEN TO VISIT
May to December
Daily 10–6

January to April
Daily 11–5

LCBO AVAILABILITY
At winery only, delivery in Ontario

THOMAS & VAUGHAN VINTNERS

Across the road from Malivoire, sandwiched between Tufford and Merrit Roads on the North side of King Street, is Thomas & Vaughn Vintners. This rather nondescript vertical pine-sided shack houses some of Beamsville's best handcrafted wines. Jason James has been making wine here since 2000. In this time, the winery has developed a reputation for serious, age-worthy, good-value wines.

It's no secret that the winery stems from a strong viticultural background. The heavy red clay vineyard that surrounds the property is where the winery sources most of its fruit. The vineyard hugs the base of the Escarpment and is well protected from damaging winter temperatures. It has been managed by second-generation grape grower Tomas Koscis and his partner Barbara Vaughan. The vines have been meticulously cared for, with many older vines producing high-quality fruit.

The property has recently been purchased by Niagara Cellars Inc., the parent company of EastDell Estate Winery. There are no plans to change production levels or the premium, small-batch standard. The new merger will no doubt increase awareness of this small, burgeoning winery.

Jason makes some scrumptious Pinot Gris. The herbaceous Sauvignon Blanc is consistently good. The Cabernet Franc is elegant, rich and award-winning. Reserve red blends are wonderful, complex and ageworthy, but pricey due to micro-production. Buy while supplies last.

4245 King Street
Beamsville ON L0R 1B1

T 905.563.7737
F 905.563.4114
W www.thomasandvaughan.com

ANNUAL PRODUCTION
4,000 cases

ACREAGE
75

WHEN TO VISIT
Summer
Daily 10:30–5:30
Winter
Wednesday to Sunday 11–4

LCBO AVAILABILITY
At winery only, in Ontario

TRILLIUM HILL ESTATE WINERY

A short drive north from Rockway Glen Winery and Golf Course, you'll see a tall white sign on the west side of Ninth Street leading you up a long gravel drive to a grand red brick home. You'll find parking toward the left side of the circular drive. The cozy tasting room is run by proprietors Ivan and Arlene Turek. Grapes are sourced from the estate vineyards and the couple's other property in Niagara-on-the-Lake. A large portion of grapes are still sold to the area's larger producers. The Tureks believe that their wine benefits from long bottle aging before release to the public. Don't be surprised to see wine from vintages dating to 2000. Ivan and Arlene want you to be able to enjoy their wines when you get them home without the need to cellar them before they reach their full potential.

The winemaking facility is housed on the opposite side of the property, in a 4,000-square-foot building. American, French and Slovenian oak are used to add complexity to the portfolio. Production is small and will stay that way, as Ivan and Arlene control all aspects of the winery and vineyard.

The Barrel Fermented Chardonnay is soft and smooth. The Chambourcin Rosé is a beefy and rugged off-dry sipper. Baco Noir fanatics will appreciate both American and French oak versions of the hearty hybrid.

3420 9th Street South
St. Catharines ON L2R 6P7

T   905.684.4419
F   905.684.3911
W www.trilliumhillwinery.com

ANNUAL PRODUCTION
2,500 cases

ACREAGE
55

WHEN TO VISIT
May to October
Daily 10–6

November to April
weekends only 10–6
or call ahead

LCBO AVAILABILITY
At winery only, delivery in Ontario

VINELAND ESTATES WINERY

As you drive south on Cherry Avenue from King Street, turn east on Moyer Road and it's impossible to miss stone-covered buildings in the distance beyond the rolling vineyards. The Vineland Estates property was settled by Mennonites in 1845. The original 75-acre property was planted in 1979 by Herman Weiss.

The winery was purchased in 1992 by John Howard. Over the span of a decade, John built the production to 60,000 cases and expanded the vineyard holdings to more than 350 acres. The export portfolio is huge for a Canadian winery. Don't be surprised to find Vineland Estates wine when travelling in the Netherlands or Hong Kong.

A patio was constructed in 1993 for guests to enjoy wines while overlooking vineyards out to Lake Ontario. The next natural step was to build a restaurant. Under the direction of Chef Mark Picone, this dining room has become one of the area's most expensive and exclusive dining experiences.

In the adjacent building, renovated to match the stonework and architecture of the original 1857 coach-house, is the retail boutique that houses a huge selection of wine accessories. You'll find everything from wine-scented candles to Riedel Crystal stemware. The whole property oozes romance, making this winery a hit for small, upscale weddings. John Howard retired in 2004, handing the reins to Allan Schmidt. Allan's brother Brian has been making wines here since 1994. Their father Lloyd is one of the area's most respected grapevine brokers. Grape-growing goes back three generations in this family; it's in the blood. It shows in the high-quality wines produced in large volume.

SOMMELIER'S PICKS

This winery has a combination of good-value and expensive wines for sale. Cabernet Franc is inexpensive and consistently fantastic. Sauvignon Blanc has loads of zesty citrus flavours. The Sparkling Riesling is one of my all-time favourite sparkling Canadian wines. Reserve reds can be extremely pricey, even by international standards.

3620 Moyer Road
Vineland ON L0R 2C0

T 905.562.7088
   1.888.VINELAND (toll free)
   1.888.846.3526
F 905.562.3071
W www.vineland.com

ANNUAL PRODUCTION
60,000 cases

ACREAGE
350

WHEN TO VISIT
May to December
Daily 10–6

January to April
Daily 10–5

LCBO AVAILABILITY
Yes, delivery in Ontario, Quebec, Manitoba and Alberta. Some products in Europe and Asia

WILLOW HEIGHTS ESTATE WINERY

Driving along King Street on the outskirts of Vineland, you'll find Willow Heights Estate Winery on the north side of the road, a few hundred metres east of Cherry Avenue. You can't miss the distinctive Mediterranean design that reflects the roots of the Speranzini family. Ron and Avis Speranzini founded Willow Heights in 1994 at what is now Birchwood Winery a few kilometres away. By the late 1990s, the winery's production had outgrown the facility and it was moved to its current location.

Ron had been a long-time amateur winemaker while working in Hamilton's steel industry until the early 1990s. After countless amateur awards, he decided to take the plunge and apply for a winery licence. You can enjoy a glass of wine with summertime fare on the winery's sunny patio.

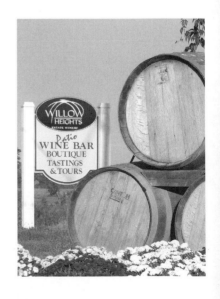

"Sur Lie" Chardonnay is a consistent buy. Reserve Chardonnay is huge and luxurious, best suited to a buttered-lobster feast. The Gamay is fresh and delicious, a great-valued summer red. Look for micro amounts of Tresette, the company's flagship red wine.

3751 King Street
Vineland ON L0R 2C0

T 905.562.4945
F 905.562.5761
W www.willowheightswinery.com

ANNUAL PRODUCTION
15,000 cases

ACREAGE
12

WHEN TO VISIT
May to October
Daily 10–5:30, Sunday 11–5:30

November to April
Daily 10–5, Sunday 11–5

LCBO AVAILABILITY
Yes, reserve wines at winery only,
delivery in Ontario

TIPS ON BUYING
NIAGARA WINES

WHAT'S THE BEST VALUED NIAGARA WINE? YOUR ANSWER WILL DEPEND ON what satisfies your taste buds.

Aromatic whites like Riesling and Gewurztraminer produce fresh, clean, intense and fragrant wines year in and year out, most for under $15 a bottle, if not under $10.

The more popular Chardonnay is also a consistent bet; however, aging in expensive French oak barrels and limited quantities can bump the price tags to well over $40. The aromatics of this wine lean toward apple, pear and mineral notes with lean, balanced acidity, unlike Chardonnays from warmer climates, which produce aromas of tropical fruit and a weighty, rich and buttery mouth feel on the palate. Good value still exists with the more fashionable unwooded versions of this great grape, responsible for some of the world's most sought-after white Burgundies.

Sauvignon Blanc continues to gain ground with Ontario enthusiasts, but pricing has crept to well over $15 a bottle due to micro-amounts of plantings. Look for the release of most aromatic whites in the spring-time following their fall harvest.

Big reds from Southern Hemisphere countries like Australia and Chile seem to dominate the market with so much variety and value. However, there's no denying that some of the world's greatest red wines come from cool climates. If you're looking for monster red wines year after year from Niagara, you may be disappointed. Niagara is likely to see three or four very hot years a decade. In these growing years, the wines' balance of fruit, tannin and acidity give them greater aging potential than those of our hedonistic, fruit-forward friends south of the equator. The growing years 1998, 1999, 2001, 2002 and 2004 were excellent in the region, so look for these vintages when consuming your red

Bordeaux-style favourites from Niagara. Most of these wines are released from 12 to 24 months from their harvest date. The best way to keep informed of what's coming up is to sign up on your favourite winery's newsletter.

Cabernet Franc may be the value underdog of the Niagara red wine scene. It's often made as a single variety and has more consistency than its bigger-flavoured and more tannic cousins. Fantastic expressions of this variety can still be picked up well under $20 a bottle.

In cool vintage years, Cabernet Sauvignon has a distinct aroma of green pepper that is a difficult obstacle to manoeuvre around for any talented winemaker. It's, however, incredibly age-worthy in great growing years.

Merlot is consistently pricey when well made, due to the grape's difficulty with handling winter temperatures. It's easy to see why wine-drinkers have a love affair with this grape, given that it's more supple and soft in its youth than its bolder-tasting relatives.

Syrah (a.k.a. Shiraz) is the industry's new favourite experiment. Some producers are labelling the variety as Shiraz, although the weight of these wines is far from the Australian style, more reminiscent of the cooler, Rhone valley wines. You'll have to hunt high and low for these scarce products.

Pinot Noir is the region's best example of caveat emptor, or let the "buyer beware." At its worst, Niagara's Pinot Noir is thin, astringent, bitter and cheap. At its best, it's lavish, sumptuous, balanced and expensive. There seems to be little middle ground the world over when it comes to the "heartbreak grape."

Icewine is expensive everywhere. Vidal is the most common variety, but Riesling is a new favourite, as its natural acidity balances the inherent sweetness of icewine. Cabernet Franc is made in micro-amounts in the region and can be twice the price of Vidal. The cost continues to climb the more exotic the variety. Many wineries are starting to offer icewines in a 200-millilitre bottle. This smaller size and price tag than the traditional 375-millilitre may give you more incentive to open a bottle at your next dinner party of four to six people. This wonderful beverage has a special-occasion stigma that producers would like to see change. Birthdays and New Year's Eve don't come often enough to keep this product flying off the shelves. The nice thing about this consumer reluctance is that wineries often have older vintages available for sale. After some time in the bottle, icewine's colour will deepen, flavours become more integrated, and fresh-fruit aromas develop a jammed and honeyed quality.

The best value in the region's dessert wines is "select" late-harvest wines. After the first press of icewine is taken, the frozen "must" is allowed to thaw for a period of six to 24 hours and pressed again. The result is a sweet wine with similar icewine aromas, one third the sugar and one third the price tag. This wine is also more accessible to cheese, pate and dessert due to its lower sugar levels and fresh acidity.

SERVING WINE
GLASSWARE
AND TEMPERATURE

DOES A PARTICULAR WINEGLASS REALLY IMPROVE THE QUALITY OF A WINE?
Again, you'll have to be the judge. Many wineries now offer a seminar to
compare a common wineglass to crystal glassware designed for specific
grape varieties. A great deal of research has been put into how the shape
of the bowl intensifies particular aromas inherent in a specific grape
variety, with the size of the opening dictating where the wine first hits
your palate. Price tags may seem prohibitive, although there's quite a
selection available now, from $10 to $150 per stem. I might suggest you
start with glassware for your favourite wine and go from there.
Remember, this exercise should improve your wine-drinking experience.

Decanting has a similar purpose. There are two reasons for decanting
a wine: sediment and aeration. Pigments literally fall out of red wine
over time and form sediment. Leave the bottle standing for eight to
ten hours. As you carefully pour the wine into the decanter, look for

sediment that will collect in the shoulder of the bottle. Stop pouring before the sediment ends up in the decanter.

Older wine may need less time to "breathe" than young wine, although young wine benefits from oxygen, too. An hour in a decanter is said to be the equivalent of a year of aging in a cellar. Next time you have friends over for a meal, pick up two bottles of the same red wine. Decant one two to three hours before your meal and open the other when your guests arrive. I guarantee they will seem like two totally different wines. Be sure to send me an invitation to your next 1978 Bordeaux tasting.

Serving temperature is also very important to all wines, from sparkling to dessert. I once participated in a blind tasting where three red wines were offered and guests were asked to make educated guesses at the grape variety, country of origin, vintage, producer, least favourite and most expensive. After all the results were in, it was revealed that they were all the same wine, just served at different temperatures. Too warm or too cold has a huge impact on the wine's profile. Unless you're a wine geek who carries your thermometer with you to your favourite restaurant, here are a few simple rules to follow. Make sure your reds aren't warmer than the room temperature. Wine that's served too warm, say from your wine rack over the refrigerator, will appear heady and boozy, as alcohol tries to escape from the glass. Some varieties like Gamay Noir take well to a 10-minute chill in the fridge before service. If condensation forms from the wine in your glass, the wine is probably too cold. The colder the red wine, the more intense the tannins appear. The colder the white wine, the less aroma, bouquet and flavour are available to taste and smell. Pull those white wines out of the fridge 15 minutes before your guests arrive, and you may discover your favourite has some new taste sensations. The same rules apply for icewine.

WINE AND FOOD
PAIRING MADE EASY

OUR PALATES ARE TRAINED BY OUR CULINARY EXPERIENCES. THE PRINCIPLES of wine- and food-pairing are simple to master. The art of creating masterful combinations is a learned response that can be explored and enjoyed over a lifetime. Issues to consider when seeking out culinary companions to wine are basic flavours, texture, method of cooking and successfully matching the weight, power and intensity of the dish to the wine.

Our tongues can only distinguish four tastes: sweet, salty, sour and bitter. The olfactory bulb in your brain can detect millions of different scents. In effect, we really smell the broad flavour profile of wine. It's these basic flavours that can complement or contrast with flavours in a dish and still work harmoniously on the palate. Freshly-poached asparagus is paired wonderfully with the grassy, green, herbaceous notes of Sauvignon Blanc. The jammed apricot aroma of late-harvest

Vidal is well-matched to warm peach pie. Pairing dominant flavours always produces positive results.

Both wine and food have a subjective texture, but, in general, lighter-textured dishes are well matched to lighter wines and, likewise, heavy foods are well matched to heavy wines. Unoaked Chardonnay made in a crisp and mineral style works wonderfully with freshly-shucked oysters, while your grandmother's roast beef may require a big, bold Cabernet Sauvignon.

The cooking method can have an impact on wine flavours, too. Steamed fish has more delicate flavours than grilled fish. Do your best to match the weight of the wine to the weight of the dish. The addition of a rich sauce or garnish like horseradish can complicate your choice. Fish served with rich sauces can stand up to fruity reds with low acidity and tannin.

Do your best to serve dry wines before sweet, as the inherent sweetness of dessert wine clings to the palate. Sparkling wines are best served before still wines, as bubbles cleanse the palate before a meal. Young wine is best served before an older, more complex wine. Lighter-style wines should be served before full-bodied wines to take full advantage of the nuances of the lighter-bodied wine.

In reds, it's important for the wine's tannin to support the creamy texture of the fats and protein in meat. In whites, acidity will perform a similar task for creamy or buttery sauces.

Now that you've got all this figured out, here are a few combinations to avoid. Vinegar is always problematic and has traditionally been one of wine's greatest adversaries. The vinegar's acidity must be matched with an equally acidic wine. Rieslings can work well.

Extremely salty food can make wine appear overly boozy, with unbalanced alcohol. A refreshing sparkling wine will best accompany this food. A classic example is Champagne and caviar.

Extremely spicy food also tends to overwhelm many wines. Heavy red wines will appear aggressively tannic, so pick a red that is fruit-forward, with fresh acidity. Gamay is a great choice. Ten minutes in the fridge also wouldn't hurt. Off-dry Riesling or Gewurztraminer may be the safest option.

The natural elements in artichokes make pairing with red wines problematic. Eggs also present problems and are best served with fruity sparkling wines, floral white wines with soft acidity, or fruity, light-bodied reds low in tannin.

Consider the seasons when entertaining. Huge red wines may not be the best choice at the poolside on a sweltering sunny day. That big red may be best served in the late fall with osso bucco.

BEST OF NIAGARA
WHERE TO STAY, EAT, SHOP AND COOK

NIAGARA-ON-THE-LAKE

has turned into a pricey destination, especially in high season, when rooms are at a premium. Find great package getaways in late fall and winter.

WHERE TO STAY

WWW.NIAGARAONTHELAKE.COM
is the best resource for accommodation, run by the Chamber of Commerce. It lists more than 200 B&Bs as well as hundreds of hotel rooms.

26 Queen Street

T 905.468.4263
W www.niagaraonthelake.com

THE CANTERBURY INN

has reasonable rates and a warm and friendly atmosphere.

170 Mary Street

T 905.468.7945
W www.canterburyinn.on.ca

THE HARBOUR HOUSE HOTEL

opened in 2003, is a well-situated waterfront property with a first-class feel to it.

85 Melville Street

T 905.468.4683
   1.866.277.6677 (toll free)
W www.harbourhousehotel.ca

THE RIVERBEND INN

was opened in 2004 by previous owners of the Prince of Wales Hotel. It offers old-world charm surrounded by vineyards at great value.

16104 Niagara Parkway
(entrance off John Street)

T 905.468.8866
   1.888.955.5553 (toll free)
W www.riverbendinn.ca

THE UPPER CANADA HOTEL
group features good-valued, well-located rooms at three small-scale hotels in the Old Town.

T   905.468.5711
    1.800.511.7070 (toll free)
W www.uppercanadahotels.com

VINTAGE INNS
The four Vintage Inns properties deliver up-scale pretense and high prices to match with the town's most exclusive rooms.

T   1.888.669.5566 (toll free)
W www.vintageinns.com

WHITE OAKS RESORT AND SPA
offers one of the area's best workout and spa facilities combined with modern boutique-hotel décor.

253 Taylor Road
T   1.800.263.5766 (toll free)
W www.whiteoaksresort.com

BEST EATERIES

DELUCA'S CHEESE MARKET & DELI
offers artisan cheese, vinegars and specialty food items. Take a grilled panini to go on your travels through wine country.

2017 Niagara Stone Road
T   905.468.2555

THE EPICUREAN
is the best stop for salads, soups and other light fare at reasonable prices.

84 Queen Street
T   905.468.0288
W www.epicurean.ca

HILLEBRAND ESTATES WINERY RESTAURANT serves great food flavours on one of Niagara-on-the-Lake's best outdoor patios with vineyard views.

1249 Niagara Stone Road
T   905.468.7123
    1.800.582.8412 (toll free)
W   www.hillebrand.com

THE LITTLE RED ROOSTER is a great stop heading in or out of town for fast friendly service and affordable prices.

271 Mary Street
T   905.468.3072
W   www.littleredrooster.ca

PELLER ESTATES WINERY has one of the most luxurious dining rooms and a pricey menu that merits the cost.

290 John Street East
T   905.468.4678
    1.888.673.5537 (toll free)
W   www.peller.com

TERRIOR LA CACHETTE Located within Strewn Winery, Terrior La Cachette is one of the best stops on the wine route serving Provençal flavours.

1339 Lakeshore Road
T   905.468.1222
W   www.lacachette.com

WILLOW CAKES AND PASTRIES is a must stop for anyone with a sweet tooth. A large window lets you view cake art in progress while supping on great coffee and individual desserts.

242 Mary Street
T   905.468.2745

THE STONE ROAD GRILL is a favourite local haunt with inventive food and a great Niagara wine list.

238 Mary Street
T   905.468.3474

BEST COOKING CLASS

WINE COUNTRY COOKING SCHOOL

Jane Langdon operates Niagara's only winery cooking school, located within Strewn Winery. Couples, along with corporate and social groups, learn cooking techniques and get help pairing wines from winemaker Joe Will.

1339 Lakeshore Road
T 905.468.8304
W www.winecountrycooking.com

TWENTY VALLEY, ST. CATHARINES AND FONTHILL

Largely undiscovered a decade ago, this part of Niagara will see an explosion in winery tourism.

WHERE TO STAY

INN ON THE TWENTY

is the leading "inn" experience in western Niagara, with spa facilities added in 2004. Spoil yourself with a luxurious getaway.

3845 Main Street, Jordan
T 905.562.5336
    1.800.701.8074 (toll free)
W www.innonthetwenty.com

KITTLING RIDGE WINERY INN

is located on the waterfront just east of Grimsby, boasting inexpensive and well-appointed rooms with spectacular views out to Lake Ontario.

4 Windward Drive, Grimsby
T 905.309.7171
    1.877.446.5746 (toll free)
W www.krwineryinn.com

BLACK WALNUT MANOR

4255 Victoria Avenue, Vineland Station

T   905.562.8675
W www.blackwalnutmanor.com

COTTAGE BY THE LAKE

5463 Blezard Drive, Beamsville

T   905.563.7434
W www.cottagebythelake.com

THE COLONIST HOUSE

4924 King Street, Beamsville

T   905.563.7838
W www.niagarabbguide.com/
    colonist-house

HARVEST GUEST COTTAGE

4101 King Street, Beamsville

T   905.562.3373
    1.866.408.9463 (toll free)
W www.crushtours.com/harvest

HOME & HEARTH B&B

3985 15th Street, Jordan Station

T   905.562.7152
W www.homeandhearth.ca

HONSBERGER ESTATE

4060 Jordan Road, Jordan Station

T   905.562.6789
W www.honsbergerestate.com

VINIFERA INN ON WINERY ROW

245 Main Street East, Grimsby

T   905.309.8873
W www.viniferainn.ca

JORDAN VILLAGE GUEST MANOR

3864 Main Street, Jordan

T   905.562.8269
W www.jmaks.ca

SILVER BIRCHES BY THE LAKE B&B

4902 Mountainview Road, Beamsville

T   905.563.9479
W   www.silverbirchesbythelake.com

WALNUT TREE COTTAGE

3797 Main Street, Jordan

T   905.562.8144

BEST EATERIES

ZOOMA ZOOMA COFFEE LOUNGE
is Niagara's best coffee lounge, with light lunches and special live music performances.

3836 Main Street, Jordan

T   905.562.6280
W   www.jordanvillage.com/zooma

THE LAKEHOUSE RESTAURANT & LOUNGE
offers a casual atmosphere right on the waterfront. Great wine list.

3100 North Service Road, Vineland

T   905.562.6777
W   www.lakehouserestaurant.com

RESTAURANT AT PENINSULA RIDGE WINERY
Enjoy the beautifully-restored Victorian Manor, with warm service and fantastic food.

5600 King Street West, Beamsville

T   905.563.0900, ext. 35
W   www.peninsularidge.com

ON THE TWENTY
Across from the Inn on the Twenty, you'll find Ontario's first winery restaurant. The elegant On the Twenty dining rooms overlook Twenty Valley.

3845 Main Street, Jordan

T   905.562.7313
W   www.innonthetwenty.com

THE MARK PICONE RESTAURANT

at Vineland Estates Winery is one of the region's most picturesque restaurants, with exquisite food priced to match.

3620 Moyer Road, Vineland
T 905.562.7088
   1.888.846.3526 ext.15 (toll free)
W www.vineland.com

VINEHAVEN BAKERY

Enjoy the handcrafted organic breads at Vinehaven Bakery, straight from Lenny and Heather Karmiol's ovens. Among the region's finest. Call ahead to reserve.

3543 King Street, Vineland
(across from Kacaba Vineyards)
T 905.562.9333

ANNA OLSEN'S FOOD & BAKERY

Can't get enough of HGTV's Sugar? Visit host Anna Olsen's Food & Bakery. Offering specialty sweets and savouries, it's a must stop when visiting Port Dalhousie in St. Catharines.

17 Lock Street, Port Dalhousie
T 905.938.8490

COACH HOUSE CAFÉ & CHEESE SHOPPE

From May to October visit the Coach House Café & Cheese Shoppe at Henry of Pelham Family Estate Winery. Open for lunch, with artisan cheese, rustic soups and sandwiches.

1469 Pelham Road, St. Catharines
T 905.684.8423
W www.henryofpelham.com
   /chcafe.html

POW WOW

has an upbeat atmosphere with creative dishes. Great wine list.

165 St. Paul Street, St. Catharines
T 905.688.3106

TWELVE-A WATERFRONT GRILL

is the new sister restaurant of On the Twenty, located in Port Dalhousie. Enjoy the contemporary atmosphere and flavours designed by Chef Kevin Maniaci.

61 Lakeport Road, St. Catharines
T 905.934.9797

THE WELLINGTON COURT RESTAURANT

has an intimate dining room with great food sensations. Small but first-class local and international wine list.

11 Wellington Street, St. Catharines
T 905.682.5518
W www.vaxxine.com/wellington

ZEST RESTAURANT

In the village of Fonthill, discover Zest Restaurant. Chef Michael Pasto combines exciting food flavours with a great wine list.

1469 Pelham Street, Fonthill
T 905.892.6474
W www.zestfonthill.com

BEST COOKING CLASS

THE GOOD EARTH COOKING SCHOOL

Nicolette Novak and her devoted team of foodies, Eric Miller and Lisa Rollo, organize hands-on and demonstrative classes on a working fruit farm.

4556 Lincoln Avenue, Beamsville
T 905.563.7856
  1.800.308.5124 (toll free)
W www.goodearthcooking.com

For additional information on locating a B&B within your budget and desired location, I recommend www.bbcanada.com.

WINERY LISTINGS

ABOUT THE AUTHOR

ANDREW BROOKS WAS BORN IN HUDSON, QUEBEC, to newly immigrated English parents. In 1980, the family moved to Calgary, Alberta, where he spent his youth in the nearby Rocky Mountains, skiing and hiking when not playing street hockey with other suburbanite children. After high school, Andrew financed his university education and trips overseas by working in Calgary's budding restaurant scene.

In the early 1990s, he met Rick Small of Woodward Canyon Winery at a winemaker's dinner. Inspired by Rick's tales of establishing a winery in Washington State, Andrew began his quest for wine knowledge. He worked in Calgary's best retail shops, wine bars and dining rooms over the next decade. Meanwhile, Andrew became a certified sommelier, mentored by Calgary's legendary wine educator Richard Harvey.

Andrew and his wife Christina have visited wine regions in Bordeaux, Burgundy, Southern Rhone, Provence, Liguria, Tuscany, Sicily, Greece, South Africa and British Columbia. In 2001, the couple purchased a turn-of-the-century farmhouse with a 10-acre parcel of abandoned orchard and vineyards in the heart of Niagara's winelands. After a painstaking clean-up process, the once-fallow land will, in a few short years, produce some of the region's high-quality grapes. The couple also created Crush on Niagara Wine Tours, a successful winery tour service that inspired this guidebook.

This guide uncovers some of the region's smallest producers crafting hidden, tasty gems. This is also the region's most accurate and current resource for highly profiled as well as off-the-beaten-track wineries. It's designed to inspire Canadians to drink more Canadian wine!